# MARCO
# TURK

**with Local Tips**
*The author's special recommendations are
highlighted in yellow throughout this guide*

*There are six symbols to help you find your way around this guide:*

*for Marco Polo recommendations - the best in each category*

*for all the sites with a great view*

*for places frequented by the locals*

*where young people get together*

**(A1)**
*map references*
**(O)** *outside area covered by map*

*for the perfect tour of the Turkish Coast follow the yellow route*

# MARCO ⊕ POLO

*Other travel guides and language guides in this series:*

Algarve • Amsterdam • Brittany • California • Crete • Cyprus • Florida
Gran Canaria • Mallorca • New York • Paris • Prague
Rhodes • Rome • Tenerife

French • German • Italian • Spanish

*Marco Polo would be very interested to hear your
comments and suggestions. Please write to:*

*World Leisure Marketing Ltd
Marco Polo Guides
9 Downing Road, West Meadows
Derby DE21 6HA England*

*Cover photograph: Fethiye Olüdeniz (Anzenberger/ Sioen)
Photographs: Lade: Binder (24), Welsh (42); Mauritius: Bartel (72), Maclaren (17),
Mehlig (45,66), Schieb (30), Vidler (21), World P./Holt (Anreise); Schapowalow: Heaton (55),
Komine (48), Sperber (32); Schuster: Braunschmid (80), Jogschies (4), Kanne (87);
Strobel (6, 11, 12, 36, 52, 59, 62, 64, 68, 71, 78, 83, 85, 93);
Transglobe: Waldkirch (28)*

*Cartography: Mairs Geographischer Verlag, Hallwag*

*1st English edition 1997
© Mairs Geographischer Verlag, Ostfildern Germany
Author: Peter Gabler
Translation: David Skillend, Mark Howarth
English edition: Cathy Muscat, Emma Kay
Editorial director: Ferdinand Ranft
Design and layout: Thienhaus/Wipperman
Printed in Italy*

# CONTENTS

# Discovering the Turkish coast

*Turkey is a land of contrasts, where East meets West,*
*where ancient civilization sits alongside modern,*
*where Islam and Christianity co-exist*

Of all the countries bordering the Mediterranean, Turkey is one of the most fascinating places to visit. It is an Aladdin's cave brimming with historical, cultural and natural treasures. Whether you want to trek inland and explore the countryside, absorb Eastern history and culture, go sailing, windsurfing, diving and water-skiing, or simply lie on the beach and soak up the sun, it is the perfect holiday destination that has everything to offer.

The coastline, which stretches from Greece to Syria, from the deeply incised bays of the western Aegean coast to the eastern Anatolian mountains, comprises more than a thousand kilometres of sandy beaches, dreamy coves, crystal clear waters and idyllic fishing villages. Inland, you will find a unique wealth of archaeological sites, dramatic rock formations, dense forests, icy mountain lakes, historic towns with colourful bazaars, and villages where time seems to have stood still.

*The old harbour at Antalya is one of the most beautiful in Turkey*

Turkey is one of the more developed countries in the Middle East, with industry and tourism growing fast. It is subdivided into two main areas. Anatolia, which constitutes 97% of the land mass, is the Asian part of Turkey. Formerly known as Asia Minor, it occupies the peninsula between the Mediterranean Sea, the Black Sea and the Aegean Sea and borders on Syria, Iraq, Iran, Armenia and Georgia. Eastern Thrace, the European sector, makes up just 3% of the country's territory (which covers a total of 779 452 sq. km). It is separated from Asian Turkey by the Bosporus, the Sea of Marmara, and the Dardanelles Strait. Bordering Greece and Bulgaria, it is the gateway from Europe to the East.

The climate of this vast country varies widely from region to region. It is largely determined by the two mountain ranges: the Taurus mountains in the south which run parallel to the Mediterranean coast, and the Pontic mountain range that stretches along the Black Sea coast in the north. The Mediterranean and Aegean coastline enjoys a pleasant climate, with hot summers and mild winters – ideal weather for the holiday season. The temperatures along the southern coast from Istanbul to the eastern border range between 28 and 34°C in summer and average at around 15°C in winter. The inland region, Central Anatolia, doesn't get much rain as most clouds gather over the Pontic mountains that form a barrier between the sea and the interior. It can get pretty icy around here in winter, with temperatures in East Anatolia dropping as low as -12°C in January. Those who prefer milder temperatures should come in the spring months of March and April or the autumn months of October and November.

The diversity in topography and climate favours a wide variety of flora and fauna. The mountains are wooded, while the interior is sparsely cultivated. The western and southern coastal landscape is typically Mediterranean, dominated by scrubland and vegetation that thrives on very little water for a long period of time. You'll see plenty of oleander, tamarisk, cypresses, olive trees, palm trees, rhododendrons, pines and *cistus albidus* – the beautiful Turkish rockrose. The water flowing down from the Taurus mountains irrigates the coastal plains, where orchards grow alongside fields of melons and citrus groves. Further east, in the fertile plain of Çukurova, vast plantations of cotton, sugar cane and bananas are cultivated, while vegetables and citrus fruits are grown for export in greenhouses scattered around the region of Finike and Kale.

The animal life is equally rich and varied. The coast is populated with many species of lizard, including the *lacerta viridis* (emerald lizard) and the frequently seen, but somewhat ugly, sand lizard. There are numerous snakes as well, but these shy creatures are often difficult to spot. At most, you might glimpse a non-poisonous adder. The mountains are home to other wildlife, including foxes, wolves, wild boar and red deer, but hunting is un-

*Watering the animals is part of everyday life*

fortunately reducing their number at an ever increasing rate, while the lynx and bear have already been virtually wiped out. You may also spot wild goats, ground-squirrels (related to the marmot), eagles, buzzards, kites and falcons. Tourism and industry still take precedence over the need to protect wildlife and the areas they inhabit; and yet the measures which have been taken to preserve the rare turtles at Dalyan show that, even in Turkey, protection of the environment and of animals is not incompatible with economic and technical progress.

The rapid development of tourism that began in the early 1970s has dramatically changed the coastal landscape. All along the coastline, hotels and resorts have spread around the small towns of Kuşadası, Marmaris, Bodrum, Fethiye and Antalya. Unfortunately, respect for the environment has not yet entered into the collective consciousness, and areas of natural beauty are still being destroyed by developers. Ecologists did, however, recently win a small but significant victory when they managed to prevent the construction of a vast hotel complex on the bay of Dalyan. They succeeded in convincing the authorities that this was an important breeding ground for sea turtles, who lay their eggs in the sand, by effectively demonstrating that the species would be endangered by the development. Half of the country's hotels are concentrated along this stretch of coast and competition between the resorts is fierce. This is advantageous for the tourist, however, as it means

there is a wide variety of activities on offer to attract custom: tennis, water-skiing, sailing, wind-surfing, trekking and tours to the archaeological sites.

The Turkish riviera is a paradise for both professional and amateur sailors. Few coastal areas can boast such favourable winds, and over the last few years Turkey has become a favourite destination for yachtsmen and sailors from all over the world. The local fishermen are now used to seeing Stars and Stripes and Union Jacks fluttering on the masts of yachts and motorboats. Fishing villages have acquired marinas, and hotels catering for watersports enthusiasts now offer special sail-and-sleep deals. Those who come to Turkey for the sailing head for the the Gulf of Gökova, or *Gökova Körfezi*, the stretch between Bodrum and Fethiye that is the heart of the southern coast. In the evolution of its tourism industry, Turkey made the development of this coast a priority, and it's no exaggeration to say that there is no other sailing area in the world which has been subject to such a boom.

But the treasures of Turkey are by no means restricted to its beautiful coastline. The whole country is a paradise for the adventurer and amateur historian. If you want to seek out the real Turkey, the somewhat harsher realities of life away from the resorts, a bus journey across the endless expanses of the Anatolian highlands, accompanied by the strains of Turkish and Eastern music, will not disappoint you.

For the explorer of things past, Turkey is a country of immeasurable historical value. This is the land where the paths of Marco Polo crossed with those of the marauding hordes of the Mongolian Timur Lenk. Noah's Ark is said to have landed on Mount Ararat after the great flood. It was here that Lucullus, the legendary Roman consul, enjoyed his luxurious banquets. Pamphylia sheltered star-crossed lovers Antony and Cleopatra. St Paul is purported to have given his first sermons at Ephesus. Agamemnon, Alexander the Great, Herodotus, Homer… all these great names are woven into a history that seeps from every crack and crevice of one of the oldest inhabited regions of the world.

There are more works of art and relics of Greek antiquity in Turkey than there are in Greece itself. Some of the largest and best-preserved theatres and ancient arenas from Greco-Roman times can be found in Ephesus, Perge, Aspendos, Side and Aphrodisias. Ancient mythology has left its trace in such wonderful relics as the fire-spitting monster Chimaera, south of Kemer. Turkey also boasts two of the Seven Wonders of the ancient world: the Mausoleum in Halicarnassos and the Temple of Diana at Ephesus.

On your travels around Turkey, you will see frequent references to the names of the small states of the ancient world. The ancient coastal region of Ionia, which encompassed some adjacent Aegean islands, was settled by the Greeks between the 11th and 9th centuries BC. During this time, Ephesus, Miletus, and Smyrna (known today as Izmir) were all thriving towns and major trading centres. The south of Ionia (the modern day districts of Aydin and West Mugla) was settled by the Carians while the region between Fethiye and Antalya was occupied by the Lycians. As a result of the natural protection this ancient province benefits from, a unique language and culture developed, vestiges of which can be seen in Xanthos, Myra, and Termessos, where the impressive rock tombs date back to between the 6th and 4th centuries BC. The neighbouring region of Pamphylia was first settled by the Greeks, but was subject to a number of different rulers until the Romans occupied it in 100 BC.

In 324 AD the Emperor Constantine I made Constantinople (Istanbul) the capital of the Holy Roman Empire. Subsequently, when the empire was divided into east and west, it became capital of the eastern Byzantine Empire. In 1453 Constantinople was conquered by the Ottomans, who had by this time gained control of much of the Eastern Mediterranean. During the 18th and 19th centuries, as the Ottoman Empire began to collapse, Turkey was at the centre of disputes between rival European powers, leading to the Russo-Turkish Wars, the Crimean War and the Balkan Wars. During the First World War the Ottomans fought with the Germans and the end of the war signalled the end of their empire. The lands were carved up among the Allies. The Black Sea Straits were rendered neutral and Smyrna (Izmir) was occupied by the Greeks.

The modern Republic of Turkey is primarily the work of one man, whose picture is inescapable and can be seen in towns and villages right across the country: Mustafa Kemal, otherwise known as Atatürk. In 1922 he led an army which was successful in its defeat of the occupying powers. On 29th October 1923, the Republic of Turkey was declared and Atatürk was elected its President. He reformed the country by abolishing the sultanate and caliphate, and replacing the holy law of Islam with a secular legal system. Atatürk was subject to fierce criticism for this from Muslims all over the world. 1928 saw yet another break from the past as the Latin alphabet replaced the Ottoman script, while in 1934 the weekly day of rest was moved to Sunday. In the same year women were given the right to vote, and in the following year every Turk obtained a surname.

In more recent years, the economic and social structures have radically changed as a result of the boom in tourism. Land prices along the coast have soared and many farmers have abandoned their fields to work in the more lucrative tourist resorts. Although tourism had been steadily increasing since the early 1980s, a series of bomb attacks carried out in 1993 and 1994 by the Kurdish guerrilla group, the PKK, resulted in a decline in the number of visitors. However, security measures have since been introduced in all the Mediterranean resorts, and great efforts have been made to make tourism safe. No attacks were carried out on any of the resorts in 1995 and, although the conflict still remains unresolved, the terrorists have gone back to fighting the government forces on the old battleground of Eastern Anatolia.

It is very tempting to make sweeping judgements about a country and its culture from quick glimpses and observations made while travelling, but appearances are very often deceptive and what the tourist sees is often a false picture, one which masks the reality of social circumstances. You will see, for example, many women in the resorts of Kuşadası, Bodrum and Antalya who dress and behave in much the same way as western women. These women are mostly from the upper echelons of Turkish society, who have come from the big towns of Istanbul or Ankara for a beach holiday. Seeing them, you wouldn't think of Turkey as an Islamic land. But the less rigid mores of the beach resorts do not reflect the rest of the country – especially not the secluded mountain villages of Anatolia. The proportion of women in academia may be higher than in some Western countries, but it doesn't necessarily follow that women are emancipated in the work place, despite what Atatürk's reforms may have led us to believe. The truth is that most Turkish women still require permission from their husbands to work. It is men who have the final say and who hold the real power, though there is a marked difference in the extent of sexual inequality between the towns and rural areas.

From the moment you step off the plane, you will be dazzled by the assortment of unfamiliar sights, smells and sounds that hit you, but it won't take long before you feel at home. The Turks are renowned for their hospitality. People will constantly invite you

# HISTORY AT A GLANCE

**c. 7000 BC**
First settlers in Asia Minor

**3000 BC**
The first records of Troy

**1800-1500 BC**
First Hittite empire

**1000-800 BC**
Greeks settle on Aegean coast

**546 BC**
Persians conquer Asia Minor

**333 BC**
Alexander the Great defeats
the Persians

**AD 395**
Division of the Roman Empire
into East Roman (Byzantine) and
West Roman Empire

**1299**
Foundation of the Ottoman
Empire by Osman I

**1453**
Conquest of Constantinople.
The town is renamed Istanbul,
capital of the Ottoman empire

**1453-1683**
Golden Age of the Ottoman
Empire

**1517**
Conquest of Egypt

**1520-66**
Suleiman I (the Magnificent) is
the dominant ruler in the
Mediterranean

**1683-1923**
Decline of the Ottoman empire.
Loss of territory in eastern
Europe. Crimean War

**1876**
Turkish constitution

**1912-1913**
Balkan war: loss of Albania and
northern Greece

**1914-1919**
First World War: Turkey fights
on the German side

**1919-1922**
Resistance by Mustafa Kemal to
the demobilization of Turkey by
the Allies

**29th October 1923**
Foundation of the Turkish
Republic. Mustafa Kemal
(Atatürk) becomes first president

**1929-1938**
Reform period under Atatürk

**1939-1945**
Neutral status during the
Second World War

**1950**
Election victory for the
Democratic Party

**1952**
Membership of NATO

**1960/1971/1980**
Military coups

**1974**
Invasion of Northern Cyprus

**1982/1983**
New constitution and elections

**1993-95**
Tansu Çiller becomes president

**1995**
Customs treaty with the EU

*Sunset over the ruins of Perge*

to share their food and drink, and you'll find it difficult to refuse. Today, many people in Turkey speak English. Even in the more remote villages there is often someone who has some knowledge of a foreign language (usually English) although it's always a good idea to keep a language guide handy. A few broken pieces of Turkish will achieve a lot. Attempting to speak the language, no matter how inept your efforts might feel, is guaranteed to break the ice. Communication will be improved and your efforts will not go unappreciated.

A characterisically proud and dignified race, the Turkish people are also renowned for their unbelievable capacity for improvisation as well as for their roguish humour. This is given perfect expression by the legendary 14th century character, Nasreddin Hodscha/Nasrettin Hoca. The comical stories about this picaresque character combine the Turkish sense of the absurd with a mischievous look at human behaviour. One of these tales relates how the author asks a neighbour if he could lend him a cooking utensil. The neighbour rather grudgingly gives him a pan, but only on condition that he return it immediately after use. On the following day, he does indeed get it back – together with another smaller one. 'What on earth is that?', asks the neighbour. 'Your frying pan has had a baby', Hoca replies. The neighbour is delighted, and on the next occasion lends the pan with far greater enthusiasm. But when, after some days, the pan has still not been returned to him, he goes to Nasreddin Hodscha and demands an explanation. The author tells him the pan has sadly died. 'What do you mean?', the indignant neighbour replies, 'A pan can't die'. Hodscha shrugs his shoulders and says, 'You believed that a pan could give birth to a child. Now you must believe that the same pan is dead.'

11

# Culture and customs

*Ottomans and Seljuks; Caravanserais and Çiftliks; mosques and hamams…*

## Alcohol

When it comes to alcohol, the rules of the Koran are not strictly adhered to in modern Turkey. Most Turks will not refuse a glass of wine, beer, vodka or raki, although moderation is the key word and over-indulgence is severely frowned upon. Alcohol is not widely available in shops, however, and during Ramadan, as a sign of respect, you should abstain from drinking alcohol in public places, especially in the rural areas, which are more traditional.

## Atatürk

The contemporary history of Turkey is closely linked to the name of Mustafa Kemal, otherwise known as Atatürk, the 'father of all Turks'. Born in Salonica in 1881, his natural ability as a military commander led him into the international political arena. He was the founder of a secret organization which joined forces with a group of liberal-minded reformists known as the Young Turks. In 1908 they unseated the ruling despot by means of a military coup. In 1915 he was successful in fighting off the allied offensive in the Dardanelles, thus liberating Turkey from foreign rule. Following the collapse of the Ottoman Empire, Mustafa Kemal set about bringing Turkey up to date. He abolished the sultanate and was elected president of the new Republic of Turkey in 1923. He introduced radical reforms, his aim being to turn the country into a modern state. He separated civil and religious powers, replacing the guiding principles of the Koran with a judiciary system. Women were given the right to vote, language reforms were introduced with the adoption of the Roman alphabet, a literacy campaign was launched across the country and the wearing of the veil and the fez, symbols of religious superstition, was banned.

By the time Atatürk died in 1938 his dreams for his country had not been fully realized. He had tried to force the country,

*Cotton is mainly cultivated in the south and west of Anatolia, providing valuable export income*

13

which had been ruled by religion for centuries, to evolve into a modern state too quickly. Today Atatürk's principles are a privilege enjoyed by the educated and well-to-do middle classes, industrialists and bureaucrats. However, his legacy has created a unique symbiosis between traditional eastern and modern western culture, which is more firmly entrenched than appearances show.

## Caravanserais

For the 13th century traveller these fortified inns, situated along the main trade routes between Europe and the Orient, were like oases. For merchants transporting precious goods such as silk, spices, china and ivory, they provided overnight accommodation and the use of a hamam and a mosque, as well as protection from bandits. A number of these spacious inns, or Hane, have recently been converted into magnificent hotels – Kuşadası and Çeşme being fine examples – with rooms and luxury suites surrounding a spacious inner courtyard which has a small mosque at its centre.

## Çiftliks

Çiftliks, once the equivalent of a moderately sized farm, have gradually developed into large-scale businesses run by rich landowners. A modern day Çiftlik is a vast complex comprising up to 15 buildings, complete with living quarters, barns and stables. Some villages are even called Çiftliks, as they really only consist of farm buildings. One such village can be found on the Çeşme peninsula.

## Circumcision

Circumcision is traditionally carried out between the ages of five and twelve, although in the towns it is often done at birth, then celebrated at a later date. The operation itself, carried out at the child's home by a trained professional, is witnessed only by women. A reception is then laid on, attended by friends and family who gather together to celebrate the rite of passage from childhood to the beginnings of manhood. The young boy is dressed in a ceremonial costume and showered with gifts by relatives and friends before being taken to bed, where he must stay until the scar is healed. There are a number of charitable organizations which arrange collective circumcisions and celebrations for orphans and poor families.

## Cyprus

After Archbishop Makarios had been deposed, by a coup d'état instigated by the Cypriot extreme right with the support of the Greek army, Turkey feared the Greek government was preparing to annex Cyprus and that the rights of the Turkish occupants (about 20% of the island's population) would be further reduced. So, in 1974, the Turks invaded Cyprus and ever since then the island, including its capital Nicosia, has been irreconcilably divided. While the Turkish occupied zone declared itself the 'Turkish Republic of Northern Cyprus' it is not recognized by the UN. Talks have resumed between the two governments, but no solution has as yet been found for the island, which lies 800 km off the Greek coast and just 65 km from Turkey.

## The Dolmuş

In addition to its buses and taxis, Turkey has a very useful and practical method of transport called the dolmuş. A dolmuş is a kind of collective taxi which stops to pick up or drop off people wherever and whenever they want, and the fee is charged according to the distance travelled. This is especially useful in remoter parts, where it would not be practical to have fixed stops. Dolmuşes are plentiful in the tourist resorts, where a system of fixed stops has been introduced along many beaches and at tourist spots. The dolmuş only sets off when it is completely full (the word 'dolmuş' means 'full') and there is never a very long wait before the next one comes along.

## Drugs

Anyone who has seen the film *Midnight Express* will not have forgotten the disturbing images of life in a Turkish jail suffered by the convicted drug smuggler. This is not mere fiction. In a country which itself grows controlled amounts of poppy seed and hemp, you may well be offered drugs, but these should be refused at all costs. The Turkish government shows no leniency to anyone caught in possession of drugs on Turkish soil. No lawyer or consular official will be able to protect you from severe punishment, nor will they be able to free you from prison before the full sentence has been served.

## Economy

Turkey remains first and foremost a rural country. Agriculture employs over half of the working population and 36% of Turkish soil is cultivated. Apart from coffee, and occasionally wheat, no food stuffs need be imported, while agricultural exports flourish. The main crops are cereals, sunflowers, olives, melons and citrus fruits. Cotton is grown in southern and western Anatolia; tobacco, tea and hazelnuts (of which Turkey is the world's largest producer) are cultivated around the Black Sea area; and raisins come from the wine-growing regions on the Mediterranean coast, where only about 3% of grapes are actually used to make wine. Citrus and tropical fruits also come from this region. Textiles, especially carpets, are another mainstay export, while coal, iron ore and mineral oil deposits support rapidly developing industries which today contribute 33% of the gross national product. Turkey's principal revenue, however, comes from tourism and foreign currency generated by the two million Turkish immigrants working abroad. With galloping inflation (around 70% in 1995), a heavy national debt, and unemployment running at 10%, the economic situation is still not very stable.

## Environment

Turkey still has no real environmental policy and public awareness is not actively promoted. There are no clear and meaningful regulations in place and a shortage of money inhibits progress. The present waste disposal system can no longer keep up with the increase in use of modern consumer goods and mass tourism adds to the problem. Short term profits always take precedence over protection of the environment. In the region around Bergama (the ancient Pergamon), for example, gold mining has begun. The people who live there fear that the highly toxic substances which are used to rinse the gold may threaten their health, and the tourism which is their livelihood, but the government still refuses to recognize the danger.

## Etiquette

The reputation enjoyed by the Turks of being a hospitable race is well deserved. In Turkey, a foreigner is not regarded as a tourist, but as a guest. You will frequently be offered tea, coffee or fruit as a polite and welcoming gesture, and one which it would be churlish to refuse. As a respected guest in a predominantly Muslim country, it goes without saying that local customs should be shown equal respect. Beyond the westernized big towns and beach resorts, avoid wearing skimpy or skin-tight clothing. When visiting a mosque, always remove your shoes and it is obligatory for women to wear a headscarf or at least cover their shoulders. During Ramadan, drinking, smoking and copious eating should be avoided in public. Take care not to photograph people against their will, as many consider it an affront to their dignity. If you are invited into a Turkish home, you should consider it a great honour, and naturally show your hosts (especially the eldest members of the family) the utmost respect.

## Europe

Turkey applied for membership of the EU in 1987, but was rejected for a number of reasons. The government has been unable to curb inflation, and there are many areas of the country which are still under-developed. The EU, already in difficult financial straits, would have to face large payment demands for Turkish agriculture. The problem of human rights abuses in Turkish prisons, as well as the persecution of the Kurds and opposition groups, are no small stumbling blocks either. In 1995, the EU nevertheless agreed to a customs union which will make trading easier, but will bring no further benefits to tourists.

## Greece

The Greeks have long been the natural enemy of the Turks. Asia Minor, the Aegean coast, and parts of the Black Sea coast had been settled by the Greeks since Antiquity. They were renowned for their enterprise and wealth, and the length of the west coast is littered with relics of the great buildings and monuments which they built to glorify their civilization.

Centuries later, the idea of a Greater Greece took root again and in May 1919 Greek troops landed in Smyrna (now Izmir). Their ambitions remained unfulfilled after a bloody war which lasted three years and resulted in victory for the Turkish National Liberation Movement led by Mustafa Kemal Atatürk. The Greeks were literally thrown back into the sea, with old Smyrna burnt to the ground. Over one and a half million Greeks left Asia Minor, and half a million Turks settled in their place. Despite these upheavals, Turkey, under Atatürk, managed to develop a closer relationship with the Greeks and even established a tentative friendship. But then in the early 1950s many Greeks still living in Istanbul were forced to flee the city following violent disturbances and, although the troubled relationship between the two countries – not least due to the Cyprus crisis – has since become less tense, the old rivalry still remains. It flared up again very recently, when Turkey suddenly laid claim to a small Greek island in the Aegean. After a brief period of muscle-flexing, however, it was decided that the island should remain Greek.

## Hamams

The Turkish bath, or hamam, came into being as a result of the strict Islamic code governing cleanliness. Each bath-house has several chambers. The bath chamber itself is normally covered by a dome-shaped roof and has at its centre a large heated marble slab. This is where you sit or lie, sweat, and get massaged. It's customary for the bath attendant – male or female – to soap and massage you. Then afterwards you simply pour ice-cold water over yourself. A trip to the hamam is a wonderfully invigorating experience, and is an absolute must on any Turkish holiday. Men and women bathe separately on the whole, but you can sometimes find communal baths in the holiday resorts.

## Holiday Villages

There are dozens of holiday villages situated along the coast between Kemer and Antalya. The standard is fast approaching that of 5-star hotels, and the Robinson Club in particular is excelling itself, both in terms of the design of its buildings and the structure of its holiday programmes.

## Islam

Almost the entire Turkish population (95%) is Muslim, mostly Sunni. The Bible, including the New Testament, is considered by

*Men in the Hamam, the traditional Turkish Bath*

17

Muslims to belong to the 'Holy Scripture'. Among those prophets recognized by Islam are Noah, Abraham, Moses, Jacob and David, as well as Jesus himself. Islam is a strictly monotheistic religion, but Jesus is not seen as the Redeemer or the Son of God. Allah, the one and only God, has no son, and so Muslims do not pray to Mohammed. He is merely the last of the prophets to whom Allah entrusted his final message, while Allah himself is supernatural, invisible, and omnipotent, as he is the creator of the world, the universe and all living things. According to the teachings of Islam, life is pre-ordained – the very word Islam means 'surrender to the will of God'. The five duties of a devout Muslim are to have faith in Allah, to pray five times a day, to give alms to the poor, to fast during Ramadan and, at least once in a lifetime, to make the pilgrimage to Mecca.

Turkey is a tolerant society and the small minority of Christians and Jews are free to practise their religion. When Atatürk came to power, he decided that the country had been kept in ignorance by the imams for too long, and set about secularizing Turkey, separating the affairs of state from religious affairs. He abolished the caliphate, closed Koranic schools and outlawed the dervish sect. But it's not that easy to eradicate customs that have been practised for 500 years. Though not fanatical, Turkish Muslims are still devout. Daily life revolves around the five calls to prayer and Ramadan is still observed.

## Kurds

The Kurds are an Indo-European race with their own culture and language (related to Persian). They live as farmers or semi-nomads in inhospitable mountain terrain between the Taurus and Sagros mountains and the Caucasus. About one third of the Kurds live in eastern Turkey, and the rest live in the former Soviet Union, Iran, Syria and Iraq.

The Kurds in Turkey have been persecuted for a long time, denied the freedom to speak their own language and live according to their own culture. This suppression led to the inevitable rise of a separatist group and today the PKK guerrillas (Partiya Karkeren Kurdistan) continue to fight for an independent Kurdistan. The government is now using its military forces against all who support the Kurdish cause, and over 6000 people have already been killed in the conflict; newspapers

### In the Marco Polo Spirit

Marco Polo was the first true world traveller. He travelled with peaceful intentions forging links between the East and the West. His aim was to discover the world, and explore different cultures and environments without changing or disrupting them. He is an excellent role model for the 20th-century traveller. Wherever we travel we should show respect for other peoples and the natural world.

**WWF**

have been closed down, reporters arrested, and villages which the Turks suspect have given shelter to the PKK razed to the ground. After an attempt by the PKK to negotiate failed, tensions were raised still further. Then in 1994 there was an international outcry when six members of parliament belonging to the opposition Democratic Party were threatened with the death sentence for allegedly making pro-Kurdish remarks. This was construed by the government as being 'support for terrorism'.

While some concessions towards the Kurdish language and culture have been made, the Turkish government still remains steadfast in its hardline approach and there is as still no end to the long and bloody conflict in sight.

## Marriage

Mohammed the Prophet declared that, 'No one, not even her father or sovereign, can force a woman of sound mind to marry, virgin or not. It is against the law'. Nevertheless, in Islamic Turkey, a good two thirds (67%) of marriages are arranged by the parents, and over half of all women marry between the ages of 15 and 17. Marriages which are based on love are rare, although this does not necessarily mean that forced marriages by the parents are the rule. A marriage is usually preceded by a lot of to-ing and fro-ing and complicated negotiation, and is not so much a marriage between two people as between two families.

## Military

The army sees itself as guardian of the Republic and of Atatürk's legacy, pursuing a strict law-and-order policy which has led it to intervene three times in the political arena, through military coups. They have applied martial law and various decrees to establish army control, and there has been widespread suppression of the opposition, arbitrary arrests and abuses of human rights. Despite the endorsement of a constitution in 1982 – later reformed in 1995 – the army still holds a powerful position in the state.

As in many poor countries, the army in Turkey recruits young men who would otherwise be in school and college. You will see soldiers everywhere, even in the remotest parts of the countryside. Generally, encounters with the military at passport control points etc. will go smoothly and not cause you any problems, but only, of course, if you treat them courteously and with respect.

## Mosques (Camii)

The word mosque is derived from the arabic *masdjid*, which means 'to prostrate oneself'. The Turkish word for mosque is camii, which means 'gathering'. Devout Muslims gather in the mosque five times a day where they bow down and pray. You'll be struck by the bareness, which is in stark contrast to the decorative interiors of Christian churches. Islamic law forbids any pictures in mosques, and thus the focal point of interest is the room itself. Apart from the area for praying (*mihrab*), which should always indicate the direction of Mecca, a pulpit (*mimber*), chandeliers, lamps, carpets, and the stands for copies of the Koran, it's the walls which attract the eye, with their exquisite and richly ornamented tiles and texts derived from, and dedicated to, the Koran.

The mosque is surrounded by a courtyard with an outer wall. It features a fountain which is used for ritual washing, and several minarets. The big mosques, especially in Istanbul, are central to a larger complex comprising *medresen* (theological schools teaching the Koran), hospitals, soup kitchens and libraries. In Istanbul and Edirne, dome-shaped mosques copied from the Hagia Sophia have become a typical feature. This form of mosque was designed to perfection by Sinan, the architect of Sultan Suleiman the Magnificent (1520-1566).

## Music and Dance

In contrast to the belly dance, which is an import from Arabic countries, the Turks have developed their own national dances and music. Typical of the Aegean coast is the *Zeybek* dance, mostly danced by men, individually or in groups, while the *Kasik oyunlari*, or Spoon Dance, is traditional to the south coast. Turkish music is fairly uniform and can take a bit of getting used to, although there are marked regional differences.

The best known of the instruments used in Turkish folk music are the *saz,* a long-necked lute; the *kaval,* an end-blown flute; and the *ney,* or Dervish flute. Due above all to the singer Ruhi Su, the folk song has enjoyed something of a renaissance and listening to his music is by far the best way to get accustomed to these new and strange sounds. Having developed an appreciation of them, you'll be able to distinguish the subtle differences between the various strands of contemporary Turkish music, which includes the usual international pop music, the *arabesque* (a type of traditional pop music with a highly ornamented melody), and more serious music, based on classical European instruments.

## Ottoman Empire

When the Turcoman nomads penetrated the borders of the Byzantine Empire, they brought with them Islam, initiating the collapse of Byzantine rule. Established in 1301 by a nomadic Turcoman prince, Osman I, the Ottoman Empire was to last almost six hundred years. After a period of consolidation, the Ottomans set about conquering new territory. In 1389 a famous battle at what is now Kosovo resulted in their victory over the Serbian king, thus extending the Empire into the Balkans as far as the Danube. To the east, they reached the Euphrates (in present day Syria and Iraq) and the Christian crusaders who tried to support Byzantium were defeated. Then in 1453, Mehmet II succeeded in capturing the last bastion of Byzantium – Constantinople. He renamed the town Istanbul, made it the capital of the Ottoman Empire and had the Topkapı Sarayı Palace built. The Ottoman Empire flourished under the rule of Suleiman the Magnificent (1520-66). Many impressive buildings were erected, including the awe-inspiring Süleymaniye Camii mosque in Istanbul. The Ottomans continued to advance deeper into the West, laying siege to Vienna in 1529. However, the wars against armies from central

*Stone relief on the amphitheatre amongst the ancient ruins of Perge*

Europe, culminating in the Second Siege of Vienna in 1683, resulted in victory for the Europeans. Various peace accords forced the sultan to concede large amounts of territory and Austria became the supreme power in the region.

The now diminished Ottoman Empire (modern Turkey, along with large parts of Greece and Albania) continued to exist until Mustafa Kemal (the future Atatürk) declared Turkey a republic in 1923.

## Politics

Turkey has for years been the only middle eastern country to have a democratic political system. According to the constitution, Turkey is a full democracy under the rule of law, with a pluralistic party political system and a free press. That said, the constitution of 1982 is the most restrictive of all western democracies and the country's per capita income is less than that of Portugal, the lowest in Europe. It's a fact that the practices found in everyday politics contradict the spirit of democracy in many ways. In 1992, a series of mysterious murders were committed, and all the victims were journalists of a variety of political persuasions. The only thing they had in common was that they had written about the Kurds. No killers could be found, and it's obvious that the press were meant to feel intimidated. After visiting Turkey in 1992, a Commission of the European Parliament strongly condemned Turkey for its daily use of torture in prisons, and it is partly this abuse of human rights which has prevented Turkey from being accepted into the EU.

Tansu Çiller, prime minister from 1993-1995, was Turkey's first woman head of government. On her resignation in December

1995, the Islamic Welfare Party became the largest political force, but no single party could form a government on its own. The military were against a coalition which would include the Islamists and, after months of negotiations, a ruling alliance was finally formed between the party of Tansu Çiller and the Conservatives.

In 1995 the constitution was reformed, so that trade unions and other associations could take part in the political process and the voting age was reduced to 18. Restrictions remained, however, with civil servants and students barred from joining trade unions or political parties. For many workers, the right to strike was completely suspended, and severely curtailed for others. Lockouts were specifically legalized, while numerous prosecutions of journalists reveal the constraints still suffered by the press.

## Ramadan

Ramadan is one of the five basic 'pillars' of Islam. It falls in the ninth month of the Muslim year and, being based on the lunar calendar, it means the dates fluctuate between 10 and 13 days each year. During Ramadan, devout Muslims – except for the old, the sick, pregnant women and children – abstain from eating and drinking from sunrise to sunset. They make up for it in the evening, however, with a huge meal as soon as the sun goes down. You'll have to be prepared for the restaurants in some villages and small towns to be closed all day during Ramadan. Visitors are naturally not expected to fast, but out of courtesy you shouldn't eat in front of practising Muslims.

## Seljuks

Originally a family of Turkish mercenaries converted to Islam, the Seljuks conquered much of Asia Minor during the 11th and 12th centuries. A branch of this ancient Turkish dynasty, the Rum-Seljuks, founded an Islamic-Turkish culture which has proved to be the seed from which present-day Turkey grew. It was the Seljuks who founded the influential theological schools, known as *medresen.* For a time the Seljuks were ruled by invading Mongols, but they were able to re-establish their position within their principalities.

## Women

You will often be confronted by the picture of women toiling in hot weather in the fields, while the men sit around lazily in teahouses. But the young, elegant and fashionably dressed women who go to work in the shops, banks and post offices of Ankara or Istanbul are as far removed from this image as their fellow female workers in London or New York. Outward appearances may suggest that Turkey is a completely male-orientated society; but in fact the proportion of women doctors, lawyers, journalists, artists, teachers or civil servants is as high as it is in the West. If women are considered to be less important than men, this has more to do with tradition and religion than with the present law. The position of women within the family itself is more complex than it might at first seem, with elder sisters, and above all elderly mothers, enjoying a high degree of respect and exercising influence in all important family matters. The social status of women may still be very low, but men treat their wives and the mothers of their children with the utmost care and respect. Public displays of affection are very taboo and the whole community, neighbours and relatives alike, keeps a watchful eye out for lapses in moral behaviour and propriety, as young girls are expected to be virgins when they marry.

## Yagli Güres

Grease-wrestling provides popular entertainment for young and old alike. The wrestlers wear only a pair of studded leather shorts and are smeared from head to toe with olive oil. The contest is won when an opponent has his back pinned to the ground. Preliminary bouts take place in the early summer, finals are held in mid-July.

## Yoghurt

Yoghurt is actually a Turkish invention and is a fundamental element in the Turkish diet. It appears in cafés and restaurants in a number of guises – as a complement to meat or as a dip with vegetables, as a dessert or as the main ingredient in *ayran,* a cool and deliciously refreshing drink. The recipe is simple, if you want to recreate the taste of Turkey once you're back home: One part (mineral) water to five parts full cream milk yoghurt; add fresh peppermint and a little salt and mix well (in a mixer if possible); serve chilled.

### Pronunciation tips and useful words

| | | | |
|---|---|---|---|
| a | as in part | ay | sounds like eye |
| e | as in pen | c | sounds like j as in jam |
| i | as in pin | ç | sounds like ch as in church |
| ı | (without a dot) is | g | as in go |
| | barely stressed | ğ | sounds like a y after e, i, ö, ü |
| o | as in pope | h | as in hat |
| ö | like the ur in purse | j | like the s in treasure |
| u | as in prune | s | as in so |
| ü | as in pupil | ş | like the sh in ship |

| | | | |
|---|---|---|---|
| hello | merhaba | afternoon | öğeden sonra |
| goodbye | hoşça kalin | evening | akşam |
| good day | günaydın | today | bugün |
| please | lütfen | tomorrow | yarın |
| thank you | mersi | one room | bir oda |
| yes/no | evet/yok | two people | iki kişi |
| sorry | affedersiniz | hot water | sicak su |
| morning | sabah | breakfast | kahvalti |

| | |
|---|---|
| I don't understand | anlamıyorum |
| I don't know | bilmiyorum |
| how much does it cost? | bu ne kadar? |
| Do you speak English? | Ingilizce biliyormusunuz? |

# Eastern entrées

*Turkish cuisine is a unique blend of European, Asian and African influences*

Over the course of many centuries, the cuisine of Turkey has evolved into a fine art. The unique variety and combination of tastes is a legacy of the vast Ottoman Empire, the boundaries of which stretched from North Africa to the Middle East and from the Balkans to Vienna. In the golden age, the sultan employed over one thousand cooks to make meals for his five thousand courtiers at the Topkapı Palace. Specialities originating from the many different countries in the Empire were prepared and adapted according to his personal taste. The European, Asian, and African influences are reflected in the wide variety of hors d'oeuvres, soups, meat and vegetable dishes and desserts that make up the modern Turkish cuisine. But all of these dishes have one thing in common: they are kept simple, the emphasis being on conserving the natural taste of the ingredients.

*Turkish cuisine is simple, tasty and above all healthy. Fresh fruit and vegetables are plentiful*

In addition to the classic national dishes, there are numerous regional specialities. Preparation methods and the degree of spiciness differ from region to region. Food is cooked with corn oil around the Black Sea coast, but along the Aegean and Mediterranean coasts olive oil is more commonly used. Dishes are spicy in the eastern Mediterranean and the further east you go, the spicier they become.

When it comes to food, Turkey is one of the few countries that is completely self-sufficient. Very little food is imported and everywhere you go you will come across markets in which the stalls are laden with home-grown and home-made produce: yoghurt, fruit and vegetables, fresh bread, honey and jam etc. As the Koran strictly forbids the eating of pork, lamb is the principal meat used in Turkish cuisine, although beef, goat and poultry are also widely eaten. The taste of lamb varies according to the age of the animal and the way in which it has been fed. The best lamb is no older than 18 months and will have been reared on thyme.

The Turkish dish we are most familiar with is, of course, the *döner kebab,* and the giant charcoal spits piled high with mutton or lamb are a familiar sight on street corners. The meat is thinly carved from the revolving spit and served in pitta bread (*pide*), fresh from the oven, garnished with onions and tomatoes. An *iskender kebab* is served with yoghurt, while an *adana kebab* is spicy. There are innumerable variations on the theme and each is equally delicious.

The real Turkish breakfast is more simple than the lavish display you might find in a hotel buffet. It traditionally consists of bread, honey, marmalade or jam, sheep's cheese, and olives, served with tea. Lunch is also quite light. The best place to eat around midday is in one of the street restaurants or snack bars for a kebab or *lahmacun,* a Turkish pizza topped with minced lamb, tomatoes, onions and paprika.

Dinner is the main meal of the day, and can start at any time between seven and ten o'clock. It is a social occasion for Turks, who like to take their time over the evening meal, which can go on until after midnight. The meal might begin with an array of hot and cold starters (*meze*) washed down with *raki* and iced water: salads, olives, *tarama* (cod's roe with lemon and olive oil), *patlican salatasi* (aubergine purée), *zeytinyagli yaprak dolmasi* (stuffed vine leaves), *lakerda* (tuna cooked in brine) and all kinds of marinated or stewed vegetables – the cook's imagination knows no bounds.

You should go easy on the appetizers, however, and leave room to enjoy the exciting soups that follow. The delicious Turkish red lentil soup (*yayla çorbasi*) is actually served as part of the main course, which is classically a lamb or beef dish. The Turks are real masters in the art of cooking *köfte* (meatballs) which are prepared using a wide variety of spices. *Tavuk* (boiled chicken) and *pili* (roast chicken) are also very popular. You can have *ekmek* (white bread) and occasionally *pilav* (rice) or *patates* (potatoes) to accompany your main dish. If you are staying on the coast, fresh fish rarely seen on inland menus, is always an agreeable alternative. I is usually served grilled. Recommended fish dishes include *kalkan* (turbot), *levrek* (bass), *lüfe* (bluefish), *palamut* (bonito, a small tuna-like fish), and *hams* (tiny anchovies). If you feel like some seafood, mussels (*midye*) and crab (*karides*) are probably your best bet.

The Turks love their desserts and the sweeter the better. The best-known dessert is *baklava* - wafer-thin layers of puff pastry soaked in sweet syrup and filled with pistachios or other nuts. Semolina dishes (*irmik*), custard-based desserts (*krem*) and rice pudding (*sürlaç*) are other common options, but if these are too heavy for you, there is always plenty of fresh fruit on offer.

The meal ends with a Turkish mocha (*kahve*), made with finely ground coffee quickly brought to the boil in a little copper pot. It is usually taken black (*sade*), and can be ordered slightly sweet (*orta*) or sweet (*sekerli*). This method of preparing the coffee always leaves some grounds in the cup – so take care with the last mouthful.

## Drinks

Çay (tea) is drunk throughout the day. It costs just a few pence and is served in gold-rimmed glasses. Sage tea is drunk a lot in the coastal areas.

To make a change from the ubiquitous international brands available, try one of the traditional cold drinks. *Ayran*, made with yoghurt, water, salt and a little mint is very refreshing. You can order it in most basic restaurants or you can buy it from the kiosks and street stands, which also sell freshly squeezed fruit juices (*meyva suyu*): grapefruit (*greyfurt suyu*); orange (*portakal suyu*); grape (*üzüm suyu*); pear (*armut suyu*) etc.

*Raki* is the third national drink after *çay* and *ayran*. This highly alcoholic spirit distilled from grape juice and flavoured with aniseed is usually taken with water. All *raki* is produced by the Tekel distillery, a state-run monopoly. There are three grades: *Yeni raki*, the most popular (and at about £1.30 a bottle in the shops, the best value for money); *Kulüp raki*; and *Altinbas*, the best and rarest. Devotees maintain that when milk is added to *raki* it is given extra power, soothes the nerves and delays the onset of inebriation.

When you see the sign *içkili* in a restaurant, it means that alcohol is sold. Wine, both white (*beyaz*) and red (*kirmizi*), has been produced in Turkey for hundreds of years. Efis Günesi (Aegean) wines are the best. They are quite dry, as are Doruk and Papaz Karasi (from the Marmara area). Beer (*bira*) is becoming more popular and the locally-brewed, light and tasty Efes is very good.

## Restaurants

Restaurants are divided into two categories; the simple *lokanta,* or the smarter *restoran*. The *restorans* offer a wide range of *meze*, main courses and desserts. Teahouses (*çay hanesi* or *çay evi*) are the places to go if you just want a drink, but these are frequented primarily by men. Women and families go to the tea-gardens (*çay bahçesi*).

There are also a number of simpler restaurants which specialize in certain dishes, indicated by their name. A *pide salonu*, for example, offers pitta bread with various fillings; a *köftesi* specializes in meat balls, and the *kebab solun* in mutton and lamb dishes. You'll find, however, that there's often no clear dividing line between the *kebab soluns*, the *lokantas*, and the *restorans*.

### What's on the menu?

| | | | |
|---|---|---|---|
| beef | *siğir* | pasta | *sirke* |
| bread | *ekmek* | pepper | *kara biber* |
| cheese | *peynir* | rice | *pilav* |
| chicken | *tavuk* | salt | *tuz* |
| fish | *balik* | soup | *çorba* |
| fruit | *meyva* | sweets | *tatli* |
| lamb | *kuzu* | vegetables | *sebze* |
| meatballs | *köfte* | water | *su* |
| olives | *zeytin* | wine | *şarap* |

# An Aladdin's cave of treasures

*Gold and silver, kilims and spices... temptations hard to resist*

The best place to go souvenir shopping in Turkey is, of course, the bazaar. Filled with clamorous crowds and ablaze with colour, it is the hub of commercial activity and a fundamental aspect of Turkish life. All the local craftsmen and women come here to peddle their wares, and the air rings with the sound of haggling and trading. Whether or not you buy anything, a trip to the bazaar is an experience not to be missed – unless you have an aversion to crowds, in which case you should steer well clear!

Bargaining is a social and commercial ritual with its own unwritten rules, the golden one being never to show too much interest in an object. Always wait for the seller to state the starting price, then offer him or her half. Be prepared for the lengthy bargaining process that will follow. Bear in mind that a final offer of below 70% of the quoted price is considered to be insulting, and it is especially impolite to make an

*Antalya is renowned for its brightly coloured, hand-woven carpets*

offer for something you have no intention of buying. It is advisable to abide by these rules if you do not wish to offend, and if you dislike the idea of haggling altogether then stick to the shops where prices are fixed.

The array of merchandise on display at a Turkish bazaar is astounding. You will find whole streets, or even entire quarters, overflowing with leather goods and carpets, jewellery and copper pots, ceramics and spices... The variety of goods on offer is sometimes so overwhelming that it's difficult to know what to buy. You should be prepared to battle against the indecisiveness that has a habit of overcoming you at a bazaar. Take the plunge and once you get the hang of bargaining you'll find it can actually be quite fun. If a merchant invites you to sit down for tea and a chat – more and more rare in the tourist areas nowadays – this is customary and is usually done in the interests of business. You are under no obligation to buy. Feel free to ask someone to show you something if you're interested in it – otherwise give a polite, but firm, no.

*Turkish crafts on display at the market in Bodrum*

More recently, travel couriers and guides have started to set up reciprocal arrangements with selected stores. This isn't necessarily a bad thing, since the travel companies have their reputation to consider and so will choose the shops they direct their clients to with care; but you should still be critical, look at things yourself, and compare quality and prices.

## Carpets

Turkish carpets are famous the world over and although it is becoming increasingly difficult to find the genuine article, if you look carefully you can still pick up some relatively cheap ones. The good quality carpets are made in Bergama, Uşak, Konya-Ladik, Yahayli and Kayseri. In Turkey, carpets are not just laid down on the floor; they are also hung on the walls. The woven *kilims* are particularly suitable for this purpose. The value of a carpet depends on its age, pattern, colour, and material. They can be made from wool, cotton, silk, or artificial fibres. The quality and type of knotting can be seen on the reverse side – if a carpet has lost its colour or become fluffy, this is a sign of poor quality.

## Jewellery

Jewellery-making has a long and rich tradition in Turkey, and there are many modern gold and silversmiths who faithfully reproduce old designs using traditional methods. Gold and silver are cheaper here (but check the hallmark before you buy) and you can find some lovely jewellery set with precious stones (again check they are not fake).

## Souvenirs

Other popular souvenirs include leather goods, ceramic, brass and onyx objects. If you want something a little different, why not buy some traditional clothing: a baggy pair of cotton trousers or an embroidered dress. For food lovers, honey (often sold with honeycomb) is a Turkish speciality, and any herbs and spices you buy here will keep for months. One thing's for sure: you won't go home empty-handed!

# Festivals and carnivals

*From art exhibitions to grease-wrestling*

**A**part from the following list of public holidays, the two big Islamic feasts of *Kurban Bayramı* and *Şeker Bayramı* are also official holidays. These religious celebrations are similar in importance to the Christian feasts of Easter and Christmas.

## PUBLIC HOLIDAYS

January 1: *New Year's Day*
April 23: *Independence Day* and *Children's Day*
May 19: *Youth and Sports*
August 30: *Commemoration of the Turkish victory over the Greeks in 1922*
October 29: *Anniversary of the proclamation of the republic by Atatürk in 1923*

## RELIGIOUS FESTIVALS & HOLIDAYS

These days are governed by the lunar calendar, and so they do not always fall on the same date.
*Kurban Bayramı:* This is a festival of sacrifice. According to Islamic religious practice, every family that can afford to slaughters a sheep during this time and offers food to the poor. (April 17 to 21 in 1997, April 6 to 10 in 1998).

*Ramadan:* The month of fasting (in Turkish: *Ramazan*). It lasts 30 days and is followed by the Feast of Ramadan or the *Şeker Bayramı* — The 'Sugar Holiday' — when everyone exchanges gifts of sweets (February 8 to 11 in 1997, January 28 to 31 in 1998).

## CULTURAL FESTIVALS & LOCAL EVENTS

**January 15-16**
★ *Efes Dove Güresi:* Camel-wrestling in Selçuk (Ephesus).

**Late April to Mid May**
*International Cultural Festival* in Ephesus. Music and dancing events; strong Turkish participation.

**First week in May**
*Marmaris Yatcılık Festivali* (International Yacht Week) in Marmaris. Regattas, exhibitions and talks.

**June**
*Festival of Watersport, Music and Dance* takes place in Foça.

*Women in traditional costume on a national holiday*

## MARCO POLO SELECTION: FESTIVALS

**1 Selçuk**
January is carnival time, during which the famous camel-wrestling championships are held (page 31)

**2 Sarayiçi, near Edirne**
The grease-wrestling championship finals are one of the highlights of the summer season. The winner becomes a national hero (page 33)

### Second week in June
*Uluslarasi Bergama Kermesi:* four day celebrations in Bergama with music and dance, fashion shows, exhibitions and theatre.
*Marmaris Sanaat ve Turizm Festivali* (Marmaris Festival of Arts and Tourism): concerts, folk dancing, theatre, surfing competitions and exhibitions.

### June 20- July 15
*Istanbul Festivali:* Istanbul International Arts Festival: concerts, dance, theatre and opera.

### Late June/Early July
Sea Festival plus an international music competition in Çeşme.

### Mid July
★ *Yagli Güres* championships in Sarayiçi. 400 grease-wrestling finalists face each other in slippery combat. The winners become national heros and are showered with fame, honour and wealth.

### 17-20 July
Armistice Celebration, *Anamur Girne Baris Senlikleri,* in memory of the landing by Turkish troops on Cyprus, in Anamur and on the Mamure Kalesi.

### 19-23 July
Antakya Festival of Tourism, Arts and Culture.

### Second week in August
*Çanakkale Festivali:* craft fairs in the market squares and open-air concerts and folk dances in the town park.

### August 10-18
*Troy Festival:* folklore festival in the historic city.

### August 26-September 10
*International Trade Fair* in İzmir: Turkey's biggest event of this kind.

### First week in September
*Bodrum Festival:* Festival of art and culture, with exhibitions, music and dance, which is well worth seeing

### Last week in September
*Grape Harvest Festival* in Bozcaada: a happy atmosphere reigns on this little island when the grapes are brought in.

### Second week in October
*Akdeniz Müzik:* international music and dance festival in Antalya.

### Third week in October
*Antalya Filim Festivali:* international film festival.

### December 6-8
*Feast of Saint Nicholas* in Demre-Kaş.

# A SHORT STAY IN ISTANBUL

(**B2**) Byzantium, Constantinople, Istanbul – the melodious sound of these three names evokes a place with a rich past and a vibrant present. The city on the Bosporus is the only one in the world which straddles two continents – Europe and Asia – and is the bridge between East and West. Although no longer the capital, Istanbul – whose conurbation counts 7.4 million inhabitants – presents a kaleidoscope of bazaars bursting at the seams, magnificent mosques and sumptuous palaces.

## VIEW OF THE TOWN

⇘ The best panoramic view of Istanbul is from the gallery on top of the Galata Kulesi, the watchtower built by the Genoese roughly 650 years ago in Beyoğlu, the Armenian and Greek quarter. The Golden Horn, as this part of the sea is called, is heavily polluted due to the lack of environmental protection.

## SIGHTS

### Aya Sofya (Hagia Sophia)

This was the most magnificent of all Christian churches from its completion in 548 AD up to 1453, when Sultan Mehmet II decided to convert it into a mosque. Today, the Hagia Sophia is a museum.
*Daily (except Mon) 09.30–17.00 hrs*

### Kariye Camii (Chora Church)

The frescos and mosaics are the most impressive feature of this abbey. The famous fresco in the burial chamber shows a vivid depiction of the Last Judgement.
*Daily (except Tues) 09.30-17.00 hrs*

### Süleymaniye Camii (Suleiman Mosque)

The mosque of Sultan Suleiman the Magnificent is considered to be the most beautiful of all the imperial mosques in Istanbul. This jewel amongst all Islamic places of worship took only seven years to build.
*Daily (except Mon and Tues)*

### Sultan Ahmet Camii (Blue Mosque)

Built for Sultan Ahmet I, this mosque rivals the Hagia Sophia. Particularly impressive is its size (it is the largest in Istanbul) and its splendid interior. The mosque takes its name from the blue Iznik tiles with which it is decorated. It is the only mosque in Turkey with six minarets. At the time of building, this number had been reserved for the holy Kaaba in Mecca – which subsequently acquired a seventh minaret. Please show proper respect for those praying.
*Daily*

### Topkapı Sarayı (Topkapı Palace)

The former residence of the Ottoman sultans (1453-1839), this awesome structure is the very image of Eastern pomp and power. Today, it is both the seat of government and the presidential home. It is divided into four courts. In the second court is the labyrinthine harem. The vast array of treasures include the holy relics of the prophet Mohammed. ⇘ This magnificent palace lies on a spit of land with gardens and

a café overlooking the sea.
*Daily (except Tues) 09.30-17.00 hrs*

## BAZAARS

### Kapalı Çarşi (Grand Bazaar)
✪ Every working day around half a million people barter and haggle here. There are more than 4000 shops spread over 200 000 square metres.
*Daily (except Sun)*

### Mısır Çarşisi (Egyptian Bazaar)
✪ Visitors entering the huge arcade are seduced by an array of competing aromas. But spices are only one line of trade next to butchers, goldsmiths, and perfumeries. The rents from the shops pay for the maintenance of the nearby New Mosque.
*Daily (except Sun)*

## BOAT TRIP

The Eminönü harbour is both the starting point for a round trip through old Istanbul as well as for a ferry trip along the coast to Üsküdur. This trip takes you through the straits, offering views of the seven hills of Istanbul and past the *yali*. These splendid, wooden Ottoman villas built right on the water's edge were once the summer residences of the aristocracy.
*Departures daily 10.25 and 14.10*

## RELAXING

◈ ✪ There is no better place to relax in than the *Yeni Camii* teagarden near the Egyptian Bazaar. The top of Çamlıca hill (the highest point on the Asian side) is also a peaceful spot and offers one of the best views of the city.

## HOTELS

### Delta Hotel
Basic hotel with no restaurant, only breakfast and cafeteria.
*42 rooms; Azimkar Sok. 3; Category 2; Tel: 212/518 56 95*

### Hilton
The hotel is situated in a beautiful park and offers all the features of a luxury hotel.
*498 rooms; Cumhuriyet Cad., Harbiye; Category 1; Tel: 212/231 46 46*

### Pera Palas
This smart and stylish hotel has hardly changed at all since the time when Agatha Christie stayed here, and the Orient Express still went to old Constantinople.
*145 rooms; Mesrutiyet Cad. 98-100, Tepesbasi; Category 1; Tel: 212/251 45 60*

## RESTAURANTS

### Abdullah Efendi Lokantası
One of the finest restaurants in Istanbul, situated in the middle of its own fruit and vegetable garden. Reservation essential.
*Koru Cad. 11, Emirgan; Category 1; Tel: 212/263 64 06*

### Sarnıç Lokantası
Gourmet restaurant just behind the Hagia Sophia. Reservation recommended.
*Sogukcesme Sok., Sultanahmet; Category 1; Tel: 212/512 57 32*

### Urcan Balık Lokantası
This legendary place is the best fish restaurant in Istanbul.
*In Sariyer, right next to the harbour; Category 1; Tel: 212/242 03 67*

# Relics of the past

*Five thousand years of history
waiting to be discovered*

Alongside Cappadocia, the Aegean Coast is the most visited part of Turkey. It is an area of great natural beauty steeped in 5000 years of turbulent history. Stretching as far as Bodrum in the Southern Aegean, it is one of the most accessible regions in Anatolia with a wellbuilt network of roads linking all the main towns. The gentle hills that roll along the coast between Çanakkale and Çeşme have long

*Remains of the wall that once surrounded Assos*

been among the star attractions of Turkish tourism. They are scattered with important archaeological sites, alternating with idyllic beach and watersport resorts. An added bonus to all this is the welcome most tourists receive from the locals, renowned for their cheerful and hospitable nature.

The area is an endless source of fascination for anyone with an interest in classical history. The 'paths of Allah' from the Dardanelles (the once strategically significant straits named after Dardanos, son of Zeus) to Smyrna, the

---

### Hotel and Restaurant prices

**Hotels**
*Category 1*: over £50
*Category 2*: £35-50
*Category 3*: under £35
Prices are for double room
with breakfast

**Restaurants**
*Category 1*: over £18
*Category 2*: £9-18
*Category 3*: under £9
Prices are for a 3-course meal
with alcoholic beverage

### Abbreviations

| | | | |
|---|---|---|---|
| *Bul.* | Bulvar (boulevard) | *Mey.* | Meydani (square) |
| *Cad.* | Cadde (street) | *Mev.* | Mevkii (district, quarter) |
| *Mah.* | Mahalle (area, region) | *Sok.* | Sokak (lane, backstreet) |

first settlement of what is now Izmir, are full of surprises – Troy, Pergamon, Asclepion, Assos… not even the Greek mainland can boast so many monuments of classical architecture.

This much-described – and well-trodden – terrain regales the senses. The coast from Çanakkale to Izmir winds along like a shimmering ribbon, offering spectacular views across olive groves and pine forests down to the sea. With its ever-changing colours, intoxicating aromas and exotic landscape, it is a most captivating place.

The downside of tourism is evident, however, in the shape of the giant hotels that look out of place here. In many places peace and tranquillity are a thing of the past. The good reputation established by the natural beauty of the landscape and the friendliness of the locals has been somewhat marred by the headlong rush to construct more and more buildings along the coast.

# AYVALIK

(A3) The picturesque little fishing port of Ayvalık (pop. 20000) is situated on Edremit Bay separated from the Greek island of Lesbos by a narrow strait. The town was founded in the 16th century (relatively recent by Turkish standards) but did not become truly Turkish until after the mass migration which followed the war between Greece and Turkey in the early 1920s. The defeated Greeks returned to their native land and were replaced by Turks from Macedonia and Crete. A certain Greek flavour remains in the quiet streets and much of the town's charm lies in its blend of the Mediterranean and the Eastern. On entering Ayvalık, you'll be struck by the pungently sweet smell that emanates from the olive presses (olive oil forms the basis of Ayvalık's economy, along with canned fish) and the pulsating life of the Ader Talat Paşa bazaar that continues as it always has. The tourist activity and nightlife is concentrated largely around the peninsula to the south of the town. Sarımsaklı has a beautiful beach bordered with hotels and restaurants. Beyond the Murat Reis Hotel, the road leads to Seytan Sofrasi, or 'Satan's Table'. From the top of the hill, the view extends from island to island as far as Lesbos and is so captivating, particularly at sunrise and sunset, that the Devil himself is said to have come here to enjoy it. On the way to Sarımsaklı, you'll come across the similarly popular village of Çamlık and the 23 islands off the coast offer numerous recreational possibilities. Also on the peninsula is a new holiday village, the Chuda Mokamp, which features a children's play area and water chute.

*4 km outside Ayvalık. 46 Zi., Alibey Adasi; Tel. and Fax: 663/ 727 15 98*

## SIGHTS

**Taksiyarhis Kilisesi**

This richly decorated Greek Orthodox church dating from the early 19th century is the only sight worth seeing in Ayvalık. Of particular interest are the pictures of Saints painted on fish skin.
*In the town centre*

## RESTAURANTS

By Turkish standards, the prices of food and drink have risen quite sharply, but by tourist standards they are still very competitive. Ayvalık is renowned for its fish restaurants where you can eat well and cheaply. Apart from the usual choice of fresh fish you can also find *kidonia* and *ayvada* (types of mussel) which are very rare

specialities in the eastern Mediterranean. On top of the list of good fish restaurants are the *Öz Canli Balik* and *Restaurant Elif 2*, both in *Gazinolar Cad* and both *Category 1*. Another recommended fish restaurant in the same street is the *Kanelo Restaurant.* It is cheaper than the latter and has an old-fashioned atmosphere. For good, well-prepared seafood in Sarımsaklı, try the hotel-restaurant *Büyük Berk, Sarımsaklı Mev.; Category 2*

## HOTELS

There are numerous small hotels and pensions in the town itself. Most of them only offer basic facilities, but they are generally cheap. The more up-market hotels and motels are to the south of Ayvalık, in Çamlık (3 km) and in Sarımsaklı (8 km).

**Artur Motel**

Very pleasantly situated on the beach, with simple but tastefully furnished rooms and a restaurant serving delicious local cuisine.
*10 rooms; Sahil Boyn; Category 3; Tel: 266/327 10 14*

**Berk Hotel**

◁▷ Above the Bay of Ayvalık, and renovated in art-déco style in 1993. Beautiful views.
*57 rooms; Ortaçamlik 23; Category 2; Tel: 266/312 15 01*

**Murat Reis Oteli**

Situated on a little bay, this is one of the oldest and most sumptuous hotels. It has a swimming pool, disco and bars. Turkish and European cooking.
*80 rooms; Sarımsaklı; Category 1; Tel: 266/324 14 56*

The Turkish communal taxis, dolmuşes, provide a constant service to the beaches. Exceptionally pretty sandy beaches can be found on the Alibey Cunda peninsula and in Sarimsaklı. The latter in particular has everything you would expect from a good resort – lots of bars on the beach and watersport facilities.

★ Boat trips are organized from the harbour on warm moonlit nights. Good atmosphere and a romantic setting.

🏃 The best disco on land is in the *Murat Reis Oteli*.

**Turizm Damişma Bürosu**
*Yat Limanı Karşısı on the left of the road to Çamlık; Tel: 266/312 21 22*

**Bergama (Pergamon)** **(A3)**
★ The regional capital of Bergama (pop. 60000) lies at the foot of the ruins of the ancient city of Pergamon. Bergama itself boasts the fascinating 2nd century Kızıl Avlu in the Bazaar quarter (12 – numbers in brackets refer to the map opposite). Originally built as a temple, this red-brick building on the river was made into a basilica by the Byzantines. But this historic site is overshadowed by one of the most famous and best preserved ancient sites in Turkey, standing on top of the hill overlooking Bergama – the Acropolis of Eumenes II.

Earliest records of the town date back to 399 BC. It became prominent following the death of Alexander the Great (323 BC) whose general, Lysimachus, had used it as his base and accumulated all the spoils of war here. It became the capital of the Hellenistic kingdom and an artistic and intellectual centre, reaching the peak of its powers during the reigns of Attalus I and Eumenes II. When faced with warring Hellenistic rulers, Pergamon was forced to ally itself with Rome and in 133 BC Attalus III ceded his kingdom to the Romans. Although it remained a prominent cultural and artistic centre its political importance declined.

The town was put on the world map in 1873, when a mosaic which formed part of the Temple of Zeus was accidentally discovered. This was the site of the famous Pergamon altar, which is now being reconstructed in the Pergamon museum in Berlin, together with part of the original frieze. You will also find here one of the largest of all the ancient libraries, established by Eumenes II to rival that of Alexandria. The Egyptians became so concerned that they banned the export of papyrus, and so the citizens of Pergamon began using animal skins for writing – and invented parchment, or 'paper from Pergamon'. They discovered that they could write on both sides of this paper, but it was too thick to be rolled up like papyrus and had to be cut and bound – and so the book was born.

You should set aside a whole day for your visit to Pergamon. The site falls into two sectors: the

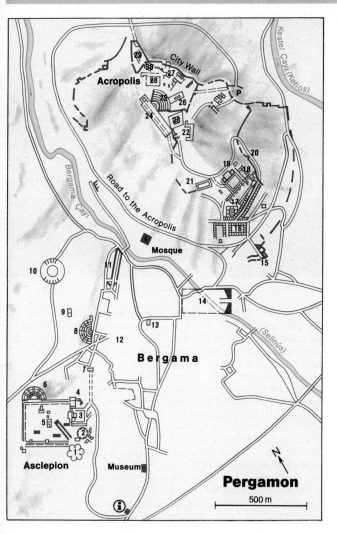

**Pergamon**

500 m

1. Rotunda
2. The Temple of Asclepios
3. Propylion
4. Library
5. Sacred Fountain
6. Theatre
7. Viran Gate
8. Roman Theatre
9. Temple of Athena
10. Roman Amphitheatre
11. Stadium

12. Bazaar Quarter
13. Ruined mosque
14. Red Basilica
15. Eumenes' Gate
16. Lower Agora
17. Gymnasium
18. Roman Baths
19. Temple of Hera
20. Ancient Street
21. Temple of Demeter
22. Upper Agora

23. Altar of Zeus
24. Ionian Altar
25. Theatre
26. Temple of Athena
27. Library
28. Temple of Trajan
29. Queen's Garden
30. Barracks

P   Car Park

*The ruins of Pergamon reflect the grandeur of Antiquity*

Acropolis and the Asclepion. The best place to start your tour is in the upper town car park. The first place you come to is the Lower Agora (16), the market square. The Gymnasium (17), where young men and adolescents were educated, was situated on three terraces, each one given over to a different age group. Not far from here the Roman Baths (18) and the Temple of Hera (19) once stood. The ancient street (20) led past the Temple of Demeter (21) to the Acropolis. Only the chosen few were allowed to take part in the celebrations honouring the goddess. Within the acropolis are the Upper Agora (22) and the remains of the Altar of Zeus (23) which once towered above the Agora. Behind the altar and in front of the theatre is the Ionian Altar (24). The Theatre (25), perched majestically on the slopes of the acropolis, is one of the most impressive of the ancient world. Other buildings include the Temple of Athena (26) and the famous Library (27). There is a wonderful view from the Temple of Trajan (28) across the site to Bergama and the surrounding mountains. The Queen's Garden (29) and the Barracks (30) can also be seen from here.

The Asclepion spa can be reached by walking through to the other side of what is now Bergama. This ancient medical centre was especially well-used in the 2nd century. People went there for a variety of cures including mud baths, massages and medicinal herb treatments. The site consists of a Rotunda (1) which welcomed those taking the cure; the Temple of Asclepios, the Greek god of medicine (2); the entrance gate – the Propylion (3); a library (4); sacred fountain (5); and a theatre (6) which is still in use.

Closer to Bergama lie the remains of the former Roman town: the Viran Gate (7); a theatre (8); a temple of Athena (9); a striking amphitheatre (10); and a stadium by the river (11).

In the town itself you can see finds from Bergama and the surrounding area in the Bergama Müzesi (museum). *Cumhuriyet Cad; Daily (except Mon)*

It is 52 km from Ayvalık to Bergama, and you can get there by bus or dolmuş. *Open daily in summer from 08.00-19.00 hrs*

## Edremit Bay                              (A3)

❖ Ören is one of the prettiest places on Edremit Bay. With its many huge pine, fig and olive trees, no other beach resort on the west coast is as verdant as this one. The narrow streets of Edremit itself are lined with wooden houses while the coastal road that runs towards Küçük-kuyu is lined with hotels and pensions offering views across the sea to Lesbos.

## Lesbos                                   (A3)

For a change of scene, you can catch a ferry across to Mytilini on Lesbos. The island is mountainous (1000 m) and covered in olive trees. From June to October, the ferries make the return journey three times a week (Mon, Wed, Fri) and the crossing takes approximately 2½ hrs.

## ÇANAKKALE

**A3)** Running between the Gallipoli peninsula and the northwestern coast of Troy, the Dardanelles – ancient Hellespont – mark the dividing line between Europe and the East. With its constant winds, a glaring sun that casts razor-sharp shadows and the bare banks of the Dardanelles rising up from the black waters, Çanakkale gives you the impression that the ghosts of history could be resurrected at any time. It's the northernmost point of the Turkish Aegean. The town lies at the narrowest point of the Dardanelle straits and has been the scene of many battles. The most recent one took place in 1915 when the city played a key role in the First World War. A Franco-British naval expedition was sent to force open a maritime passage, the intention being to seize Istanbul and establish a link with Russia. After having lost one third of their fleet in a bloody battle, the Allies were forced to retreat. The Turkish troops were led by a young Mustafa Kemal who was later to become a national legend. The military museum in the Sultaniye-Kalesi exhibits relics from the various battles that took place here.

The town's main importance today is as a cross-over point for maritime traffic between the European and Asian parts of Turkey. Although shrouded in legend and history, there are few sights worth seeing here today, largely because the town and its surroundings were devastated by an earthquake which struck in 1912.

Çanakkale benefits from the tourism generated by the close proximity of Troy. The image of the Trojan Horse which you'll see stamped on all brochures and packaging is now also the official logo of the town.

## SIGHTS

### Sultaniye Kalesi

The Ottoman castle was built in 1462-63 by Mehmet II. Its two fortresses enabled the Turks to control traffic passing through the narrowest point of the Dardanelles. The structure proved crucial when the Allies tried to force their way through in 1915. It now houses a Military museum in which you can see exhibits from the Dardanelles battles.

*Daily (except Mon) 09.00-12.00 and 13.30-17.30 hrs*

## MUSEUM

### Çanakkale Arkeoloji Müzesi (Archaeological Museum)

Finds and discoveries mainly from Troy and Dardanos. Especially worth seeing are the gold and jewellery excavated from the graves and the King's Tomb.

*Daily (except Mon) 08.30-16.30 hrs*

## RESTAURANTS

*L'Entellektüel (Rihtim Cad.)* and the *Yalova Liman (Kordon Boyu)* are two of the best restaurants in town. Both serve excellent fish dishes which can be enjoyed on the terrace while taking in the view of the strait.

*Category 2*

## HOTELS

### Anafartalar Hotel

Large hotel by the quayside. All rooms facing the sea have a balcony. ❖ You can watch the ships pass through the strait from the roof-terrace restaurant. The view is particularly impressive at night. Very friendly and efficient staff.

*70 rooms; Kayserili Paşa Cad.; Category 2; Tel: 286/217 44 54*

### Büyük Truva Hotel

Quieter, though not as comfortable as the Anafartalar Hotel.

*66 rooms; Yaliboyn Cad; Category 2, Tel: 286/217 104*

### Tusan Hotel

This comfortable hotel overlooking the sea nestles beneath shady trees 14 km south of Çanakkale. Private beach. All rooms have balcony or terrace.

*64 rooms; P.k. 8 Intepe; Category 2, Tel: 286/232 82 73*

---

### The male prerogative

Men-only restaurants and bars are still an integral part of Turkish culture. In some establishments, women who dare enter are ushered into separate rooms, or else seated on a different floor altogether. Whether they agree with it or not, women tourists should be sensitive to this custom and comply with local tradition so as to avoid any unnecessary misunderstandings. If no separate room is available, this doesn't necessarily mean that women are forbidden to enter, but in such a situation, they should try to sit at a distance from the male groups in a separate corner. There are, of course, plenty of places where these eastern rules don't apply – particularly in tourist resorts and restaurants.

*Few ruins in Troy are as well-preserved as the ancient theatre*

## SPORT & LEISURE

The most beautiful beaches in the region can be found on the islands of Bozcaada and Gökçeada in the Dardanelles. There are daily ferry crossings between Çanakkale and Odunluk. You can also bathe along the beaches of Kilitbahir on the European side of the Dardanelles. During the high season, there are boat trips across to Eceabat every hour. The journey time is approximately 30 minutes.

## INFORMATION

**Turizm Danişma Bürosu**
*Iskele Mey. 67; Tel: 286/217 11 87*

## SURROUNDING AREA

**Assos** **(A3)**
Assos lies at the head of the Gulf of Edremit. Founded in 1000 BC by the Aeolians, Assos was successively ruled by the Lydians, the Persians, the Pergamons, the Romans and the Byzantines. Despite the passage of so many different cultures, it never played any significant historical role (although it is said to have been visited by Aristotle and Saint Paul) and was always under the shadow of Troy. The fortifications that surround the town are, nevertheless, quite impressive. There is a fine view from the acropolis across the azure sea to the island of Lesbos 10 km away. Assos can be reached by dolmuş or there is a daily bus service from Çanakkale. The journey takes about two hours.

**Halicilik Okuluve Kooperatifi (School and Cooperative for Carpet Making)** **(A3)**
★ The carpets woven and knotted in this cooperative are unique in both design and quality. A visit to the workshop gives an interesting insight into the ancient craft. Carpets are also sold here at extremely favourable prices.
*In Ayvacik, 18 km south of Çanakkale*

## Troy (A3)

The architectural remains of the town of Homer's *Iliad* are sparse. Countless hypotheses based on the epic have been put forward, but none can verify irrefutably that the Trojan War actually took place. According to the Greek legend, Paris, son of Priam, abducted Helen, wife of the Spartan king Menelaus, who was reputed to be the most beautiful woman in the world. Agamemnon, the king's brother, was sent to retrieve her. The ensuing war lasted ten years and ended in Greek victory over Troy, thanks to the legendary wooden horse strategem devised by Odysseus. Remains of the city of Troy were discovered by Heinrich Schliemann (1822-1890), a German amateur archaeologist who is thought to have disturbed many valuable artefacts with his over-enthusiastic digging. The Treasure of Priam mysteriously disappeared during the Second World War (reappearing some 50 years later in Russia) and, apart from the 20 m-high gimmicky wooden horse built with American backing, there's scarcely anything left to be seen of Homer's Troy. It's really the atmosphere, more than the ruins, which provides the charm of the place. Many travel agencies operate tours of Troy (*eg: Troy-Anzac in the Saat Kulesi Yani 2*).

*Open daily from sunrise to sunset; Entrance £3.00 approx.; Taxi from Çanakkale costs £7.50 approx., excursion to Troy lasts around 4 hrs*

## Bozcaada (0)

★ According to legend, it was behind this island that Agamemnon and his fleet lay in wait, while the Trojans transported the wooden horse they had left on the beach into the city. It is a small island full of charm and popular with local holiday-makers. Surrounded by golden sands and crystal clear waters (the prettiest beaches are in the south and south-west) it is a perfect place for bathing. Basic accommodation is available from £6.00 a night. The majority of restaurants (predominantly fish) are along the harbour. Bozcaada can either be reached from Çanakkale (3 hrs) or from Odunluk, approximately 60 km south of Çanakkale.

## Gökçeada (0)

★ This relatively large island is a pretty place with wild lonely beaches, clear water and plenty of opportunities for walking. The crossing from Çanakkale takes 3 hrs (departure daily at 16.00 hrs). The island is not equipped for mass tourism, but there are quite a few campsites and family pensions. Two reasonable hotels are the *Ada Oteli* in the town (*Tel 1967/10 75*) and the *Ayan Oteli* by the harbour (*Tel: 1967/11 36*).

# ÇEŞME

(A4) ♨ This former fishing village (pop. 10 000) on the western tip of Turkey is one of the most popular resorts on the Aegean. The symbol of the town is its castle. Built by the Genoese in the 15th century it directly overlooks the harbour. Çeşme is also known for its two hot springs, şifne and Ilıca, the water from which is piped directly to most of the hotels. Some hot springs bubble up from the sea bed in Boyalik Bay, and swimming here feels a bit like taking a hot bath.

## SIGHTS

**Silah Müzesi (Weapons Museum) and Castle**
Here you can see selected items from the collection in the Topkapı museum in Istanbul – ship cannons and other defences. There is also a lovely view from here over the whole harbour.
*The castle is open daily in summer, 08.00-12.00 and 13.00-17.30 hrs; Entrance 50p approx.*

## RESTAURANTS

Food and accommodation in Çeşme is not cheap. The best restaurants are on the harbour.

**Buhara Et Lokantası**
This restaurant specializes in meat dishes, served with home-made bread. Good quality at reasonable prices.
*By the castle; Category 3*

**Sahil Lokantası**
Popular tourist restaurant on the harbour, serving mostly fish.
*Cumhuriyet Mey.; Category 2; Tel: 232/712 16 46*

## SHOPPING

The shopping streets are dominated by jewellery, leather goods and carpets. There are a number of shops selling Ottoman antiquities, but prices tend to be high.

## HOTELS

**Arinnanda Hotel**
Pretty little hotel with a pleasant atmosphere. Old bar and Turkish bath. 3 km from Çeşme, in Ilica.
*56 rooms; Boyalik Mev.; Category 1; Tel: 232/723 45 00*

**Çeşme Marin Hotel**
Pleasant, small hotel on the promenade.
*20 rooms; Hürriyet Cad. 10; Category 2; Tel: 232/712 64 84*

**Framissima Boyalik Beach Hotel**
The best hotel, situated right on the beach. Two restaurants serving Turkish and European specialities.
*210 rooms; Boyalik; Category 1; Tel: 232/712 70 81*

**Kanuni Kervansaray Hotel**
Formerly a caravanserai, this luxury inn has a wonderful atmosphere. In its idyllic inner courtyard, where exhausted camels once rested, tourists now unwind.
*34 rooms; Category 1; Tel: 232/712 64 90*

**Turban Ilica Hotel**
Beautiful hotel; good cuisine.
*65 rooms; Dereboyu Mev. Boyalik; Category 2; Tel: 232/712 21 28*

## SPORT & LEISURE

There are lots of lovely beaches, but the 'golden sand' of *Altinkum/Tursite* is the longest and most beautiful one on the peninsula. The clear waters around Çeşme are particularly good for diving. Before planning a diving trip, you should find out from the tourist office which are the authorized sites, as diving near shipwrecks is not permitted.

## ENTERTAINMENT

All the action is in Ilica. Disco prices have now reached European levels. The best venue is the *Altinyunus Disco* which is pleasantly situated on a little hill.

**Turizm Danişma Bürosu**
*Iskele Mey. 8 by the quay; Tel: 232/712 66 53*

## SURROUNDING AREA

### Chios (A4)

In the summer car ferries cross daily from Çeşme to the Greek island of Chios. The crossing takes one hour and costs approx. £17.00 per person. Sakiz – as the Turks call it – boasts a number of beautiful beaches.

# IZMIR

**(A4)** İzmir (pop. 2 million) is Turkey's third largest city after Istanbul and Ankara. Its new airport, two railway stations, bus station and new port make it an ideal base from which to explore. The ancient town of Smyrna was considered to have been one of the most beautiful in the world. Smyrna was once the main trading centre of the eastern Mediterranean. Businesses were established here and huge fortunes made – and of course local customs and morals were more relaxed too. In 1922, the whole of the old town was devastated by fire, and little of old, cosmopolitan Smyrna is left to be seen.

Today, İzmir is still an important commercial centre. Liberal attitudes prevail – the people are very open and receptive to new ideas. İzmir isn't a place to which tourists flock – it's loud and smoggy and is short on historical sites and monuments. The town is typical of a modern Turkish metropolis; but for some, this could be a good reason to spend time here. Note that only the main streets have names, all others are designated numerically.

*The Clock tower (Saat Kulesi) is the official symbol of Izmir*

## SIGHTS

### Agorá

Numerous excavations have uncovered the site of İzmir's agora (the ancient Roman market place). Part of a collonade is still standing and you can see the remains of a basilica with three naves as well as some beautiful Ottoman gravestones.

*Daily (except Mon) 09.00-12.00 and 13.30-17.30 hrs; Gaziosmanpasa Bul.*

### Kadifekale (Velvet Castle)

◆ The view from the Velvet Castle on Pagos hill sweeps across much of the town, taking in the *geçekondu* – the slums in the east – the harbour in the north and the old suburbs of Karsiyaka and Bayrakli. The castle ramparts, which date back to the 3rd century BC, are among the few vestiges of the Roman era.

### Konak Meydanı

◈ This vast square is the life and soul of İzmir, with its clock tower, government offices, cultural centres and hospitals, dozens of bus stops and nearby jetties. It serves as a central meeting point for people from the neighbouring commercial districts.

### Kültür Parkı

The biggest recreational area in the centre of the town lies between the Basmane and Alsancak quarters and covers the area of the old town destroyed by the 1922 fire. A wide variety of entertainment is on offer day and night. There's a small zoo, a parachute tower, an artificial lake, two theatres, a tea-garden, tennis courts, swimming baths, and some restaurants and nightclubs.

### Saat Kulesi (Clock Tower)

The clock tower, official symbol of İzmir, is a fine example of late Ottoman architecture. It was built in 1901 to mark the 50th anniversary of Sultan Abdülhamid II's accession to the throne.
*Konak Mey.*

## MUSEUMS

### Arkeoloji Müzesi (Archaeological Museum)

A visit to the modern museum above the Konak Mey is a must. Exhibits include important finds from the ancient sites of the Aegean, marble statues and ritual burial objects.

*Daily (except Mon) 09.00-12.00 and 13.00-17.00 hrs; Entrance approx. £1.50; Birlesmis Milletler Yokusu*

### Atatürk Müzesi

This is the building in which Atatürk stayed during his visits to Izmir. It now houses a museum dedicated to his memory.

*Daily (except Mon) 09.00-12.00 and 13.00-17.00 hrs; Entrance approx. 20p; Atatürk Cad. 248*

### Resim ve Heykel Müzesi (Painting and Sculpture Museum)

Contemporary Turkish painters and sculptors display their work here.

*Daily (except Sat and Sun) 10.00-17.00; Konak Mey*

## RESTAURANTS

### Deniz Restaurant

◈ Very good, typical Turkish restaurant, known for its fish specialities. Frequented by families and business people alike.

*Atatürk Cad. 188; Category 2; Tel: 232/422 06 01*

### Eighteen Eighty Eight (1888)

⚘ Elegant restaurant with bar in a typical old İzmir-style house built in 1888 with an exotic garden. Turkish and Mediterranean cooking, with live music on Wednesdays and at weekends.
*Cumhuriyet Bul. 248; Category 1; Tel: 232/421 66 90*

### Kemal's Place

A 50-year-old tavern which has won numerous awards for its gastronomic prowess. A speciality is fish cooked in milk.
*1453 Sok. 20/A; Category 2; Tel: 232/422 31 90*

### Kismet

Recommended in this smart restaurant are the Russian specialities and the 'Kismet kebab'.
*1377 Sok. 9; Category 1; Tel: 232/463 38 50*

### Sarap Evi

This rustic restaurant is renowned for its steaks and Turkish grill specialities.
*In the Kültür Parkı; Category 3; Tel: 232/483 47 87*

---

## SHOPPING

### Bazaar District

★ At the intersection between the *Anafartalar Cad.* and the *945* is one of the best spots in old İzmir. In the *Akbeki Hotel*, you can still see men smoking their traditional water pipes, while in the cafés around the Hatuniye mosque you can enjoy a traditional Turkish mocha. The Anafartalar Cad. the economic artery of the town, runs through the huge Kemeraltı bazaar, one of the most beautiful in Turkey and worth visiting particularly for gold and jewellery.

The most elegant shops are situated between the Cumhuriyet Mey and the jetty of Alsancak.

### Bitpazari (Fleamarket)

A real treasure trove of bric-a-brac and second-hand goods. A great place for browsing and rummaging. It's open daily, but is especially lively on Sundays.
*In the 1369 Sok.*

### Döner Sermaye Müdürlügü

The first state-controlled souvenir shop. Haggling is forbidden here – a unique phenomena in Turkey!
*In the Cumhuriyet Mey., around the corner from the Büyük Hotel*

### Ilhan Nargile

Shop specializing in water pipes. These are no objets d'art; they are purely functional. Small ones on sale from as little as £13.00.
*Asil Han, 856 Sok. 7/c*

---

## HOTELS

### Büyük Efes Hotel

The largest and most beautiful luxury hotel in İzmir. In the evenings, the restaurant tables are set up around the swimming pool. There is a popular Hamam which is also open to paying non-residents. ❸ The hotel disco and night-club are a popular place for the smart set of İzmir to meet.
*446 rooms; Gaziosmanpasa Bul., Category 1; Tel: 232/484 4300*

### Hilton

The second largest and most modern hotel in İzmir which fully meets Hilton standards. ◣ Panoramic bar.
*81 rooms; Category 1; Gaziomanpaşa Bul. 7; Tel: 232/441 60 60*

## Karaca Hotel

Pretty mid-range hotel with an American Bar and a small swimming pool on the roof terrace.
*69 rooms; 1379 Sok. 55; Category 2; Tel: 232/489 19 40*

Since the water around İzmir is highly polluted, you would do better to pamper yourself in a Turkish bath than swim in the sea. The best is in the *Hotel Büyük Efes, Gaziosmanpaşa Bul. 1.*

## Bohem Disco

✠ Frequented by İzmir's rich kids. Spirited atmosphere; dancing till dawn.
*From 22.00 hrs; by the harbour*

## Charli Bar

Stages the occasional live jazz performance.
*1387 Sokak 3*

## Santana Paviyonu

Renowned night club featuring belly dancing and striptease.
*Entrance free; from 22.00 hrs; Kazimpaşa Bul. 16*

## Turizm Danişma Bürosu

*Gaziosmanpaşa Bul. 1166; Tel: 232/484 21 47*

## Balçova                    (A4)

The biggest thermal centre in Turkey was already a spa in ancient times. The hot springs (40°C) are perfect for a number of ailments – they help with the cure of skin diseases, rheumatism and breathing problems.

## Foça                       (A4)

✠ Present day Foça (pop. 10 000) is a vibrant holiday resort with two small bays, a peninsula and a castle. The prettier beaches are in Yeni Foça (New Foça). Foça itself lies on the site of ancient Phocaea, founded in the 8th century BC. A little outside the town is the *Hotel Leon, Birinci Mersinaki, Karacina Mev.; 68 rooms; Category 2; Tel: 232/812 29 60.* In an old Greek villa is the *Hotel Karacam; 22 rooms; Category 2; Tel: 232/812 14 16; by the harbour*

## Gümüldür                   (A4)

This village has devoted itself to tourism, its only asset being a long sandy beach and crystal clear water. Quite a few hotels and holiday villages (*Club Yali; Tel: 232/793 14 07*) have been built here.

## Manisa                     (A-B3)

The provincial capital (pop. 100 000) not only has pre-Ottoman and Ottoman architecture, but exquisite delights for the palate, too. Try the *mesir macunu,* a type of vol-au-vent, which is made from over one hundred ingredients. A little road behind the Muradiye mosque leads up to the Weeping Rock of Niobe where legend has it that Niobe taunted the nymph Leto and saw her twelve children killed as a result.

## Teos                       (A4)

◁▽▷ A visit here is another must to see the remains of the Temple of Dionysus, built to worship the tutelary God of Teos, the theatre, and the Roman odeum, all set against wonderful coastal scenery.

# A turquoise cruise

*Exploring the treasures of Antiquity
and cosmopolitan beach resorts*

The southern Aegean coast stretches from Çeşme to the Bay of Marmaris and broadly covers the territory of the ancient Greco-Roman kingdom of Caria. The region boasts a whole array of attractions, from superb beaches to sites of classical Antiquity, and traditional fishing villages to vibrant tourist resorts. The stadium at Ephesus is the best preserved ancient city in the whole of the Mediterranean and every January an unmissable event is staged here: the national camel-wrestling championships; *Dove Güresi*. Other important historical sites, such as Priene, Aphrodisias and Milet, are to be found along the winding valley of the Büyük Menderes Nehri. You can bathe in the hot springs at the natural wonderland of Pamukkale, or else pick your way through the ruins of the Mausoleum at Halicarnassos, one of the Seven Wonders of the Ancient World. The turquoise coast is ideally suited to the

*The ancient city site of Ephesus transports you to the past*

watersports enthusiast, with Bodrum and Marmaris the centres for the yachting fraternity.

## BODRUM

**(B5)** ☃ In the 1950s, Bodrum was still a quiet little fishing village, albeit one with a 3000 year history. It remained largely undiscovered until the Istanbul jet-set adopted it and turned it into a thriving holiday resort, which was soon brought up to international standards. Its Côte-d'Azur chicness now attracts an increasing number of foreign tourists .

There are now only a few reminders of the quaint charm of the old town, with its white-washed houses dotted across the terraced hillsides, the lovely little back streets with views over the breathtakingly beautiful bay, and a harbour crowded with countless yachts and fishing boats. The bathing season lasts from April until October and the town boasts a vibrant nightlife.

In ancient times, this was the site of Halicarnassos. The Carian ruler Mausolus (377-353 BC) made the town the capital of his empire and built the splendid Halicarnassos Mausoleum, which his wife Artemisia II completed for him after his death. The word has since passed into general usage to describe any large and grandiose tomb. Little remains of the building itself, as the huge slabs of stone were later used to build the castle and the town wall. Bodrum's most famous son, the scholar Herodotus (490-425 BC), was the first to chronicle the old town's history.

One cannot help but wonder how a small town of 30 000 inhabitants manages to accommodate 200 000 visitors during the holiday period. At the height of the season, it often feels as if half of Europe has come here on holiday, and you may find it difficult to escape the crowds.

## SIGHTS

### Bodrum Kalesi
### (The Castle of St Peter)
This 15th century castle, along with its museum, towers above the port. It was built in part with stones from the Mausoleum, plundered by the Knights of St John for their stronghold. Situated right by the harbour entrance, the building has become the official symbol of the town.

## MUSEUM

### Bodrum Sualti Arkeoloji Müzesi
### (Museum of Underwater Archaeology)
This unusual museum in the walls of the castle houses some fascinating underwater finds, some of which date back to the 14th century BC. Among the many exhibits is the cargo of a Byzantine ship (containing amphorae, coins and weapons, etc.), which was discovered and salvaged in 1977.
*Daily (except Mon) 09.00-12.00 and 13.00-17.00 hrs; in the Bodrum Kalesi*

## RESTAURANTS

Bodrum is famous for its charcoal grilled *köftes* – spicy meatballs served on skewers. There are plenty of good restaurants pleasantly situated by the harbour.

### Ahtapot
Squid and octopus are the specialities of this restaurant.
*Atatürk Cad.; Category 2*

### Amphora
Pleasant restaurant on the marina with good food.
*Neyzen Tevfik Cad.; Category 2; Tel: 252/316 23 68*

### Han
Large selection of *mezeler* and fish… and belly dancing.
*Kale Cad.; Category 1; Tel: 252/316 16 15*

## SHOPPING

The shopping streets are towards the castle and Atatürk Cad. and while a wide range of goods is on offer, the place is not exactly cheap. All kinds of leather goods can be bought here. Natural sponges are sold cheaply, but remember that they are an endangered species.

## HOTELS

The hotel infrastructure of Bodrum is well-developed and there

## MARCO POLO SELECTION: SOUTHERN AEGEAN

**1 Ephesus**
The most imposing and well-preserved ancient settlement in Asia Minor (page 62)

**2 Gulf of Gökova**
One of the loveliest bays in the Gulf of Gökova is Akbük, by Ören, south of which lies Cleopatra's Island (page 56)

**3 Sailing at Marmaris**
Escape the hustle and bustle of Marmaris on a relaxing boat trip along the Lycian coast (page 67)

**4 Pamukkale**
Beyond the ancient city of Hierapolis, a petrified waterfall shines a dazzling white in the sun (page 64)

is a wide range of accommodation on offer, from the most basic pension to the most luxurious holiday village.

### Aksu Hotel
Good family hotel with a roof-terrace and swimming pool.
*24 rooms; Cumhuriyet Cad. 155; Category 2; Tel: 252/316 18 33*

### Halikarnas Hotel
Luxurious and busy hotel in pleasant surroundings.
*30 rooms; Cumhuriyet Cad. 128; Category 1; Tel: 252/316 80 00*

### Milta Torba
Lovely holiday complex with many recreational facilities. Can accommodate approximately 800 people.
*352 rooms; 7 km outside Bodrum; Kizilagac Mev.; Category 1; Tel: 252/316 23 43*

### Monastir Hotel
Superb hotel above the bay which affords a wonderful view. Swimming pool and tennis court.
*51 rooms; Baris Sitesi Mev.; Category 1; Tel: 252/316 28 54*

### SPORT & LEISURE

There is excellent windsurfing in and around Bodrum, particularly in the afternoons when the sea breeze gets up. Gümbet bay, west of Bodrum, attracts windsurfers from all over the world. You can try your hand at almost any watersport here — windsurfing, sailing, diving, waterskiing and even parascending.

With over 1000 boats available for hire, yacht charter is the main source of income for Bodrum. The bigger boats all come with crew, and prices vary depending on the season, boat facilities and the number of passengers, but you should reckon on paying at least £250 per person.

Charter addresses: *Kemal Bilen, Frkateyin Sok. 17; Tel: 252/316 16 03* or *Ebrahim Göl, Turgutreis Cad. 11; Tel: 252/316 49 49.* Travel agencies abroad can also arrange yacht hire.

### ENTERTAINMENT

Nightlife in Bodrum continues into the early hours and the main rendezvous is on the promenade alongside the yacht marina.

## Hadigari Bar and Disco

☆ Best bar in town.
*Dr. Alim Bey Cad.*

There is a variety of clubs on the *Cumhuriyet Cad.*:

## Halikarnas Disko

☆ This open air disco is considered to be one of the best in the world. Bands start playing as late as four o'clock and carry on till dawn.

## Kavalye Bar

Intimate atmosphere late into the night.

## Lodos Bar

Good crowd and a great atmosphere.

---
**INFORMATION**
---

**Turizm Danişma Bürosu**
*12 Eylül Mey.; Tel: 252/316 10 91*

---
**SURROUNDING AREA**
---

### Euromos                          (B4)

The Temple of Zeus is a fine example of Corinthian architecture and one of the best preserved in Asia Minor. Not far from Milâs and definitely worth a visit.
*Approx. 60 km north of Bodrum on the N.330*

### Gökova Gulf                      (B5)

★ Bodrum is one of the departure points for a *mavi yolculuk*, or 'turquoise cruise' along this beautiful stretch of coast. The Gökova Gulf is 56 km long, with the prettiest and most interesting places within a 32 km-wide strip

on the north-east coast of the Resadiye peninsula. What was once a trip in a sponge-diving boat is now a luxury voyage in a *gulet*, the typical broad-beamed Turkish two-master.

One of the loveliest coves is Akbük, immediately behind Ören. South of Akbük lies Cleopatra's Isle. The beach here is barely 20 m long and just 3 m wide, and legend has it that Mark Antony brought the sand here specially, all the way from the Nile – the Turks are so proud of this that it's forbidden to take a single grain of sand home with you as a souvenir.

Since boats with day-trippers seem to block the cove all day, charterers would be advised to anchor off the cove in the late afternoon, putting out to sea again at about 10.00 hrs the following morning. You can book a 'turquoise cruise' from most of the yachting and charter companies in Bodrum harbour. Depending on the size of the boat and its facilities, a trip costs between £440 and £660 per person per week.

### Kos                              (B5)

A trip to Kos, the Greek island in the Sporades, is worth making not only for its beautiful beaches, but also for its range of interesting walks.
*Departures daily at 09.00 hrs from the harbour, return 16.30 hrs; £15 per person*

---
# DATÇA
---

(B5) The narrow Resadiye peninsula stretching away to the west marks a clear dividing line between the Aegean and the

Mediterranean. Until only a few years ago, Datça was still a quiet little fishing port off the beaten track, but now yachting tourists have woken the village from its slumbers. While there are no sites of historical interest, holidaymakers come here to relax and enjoy the beautiful beaches, rocky coves, and a wide range of hotels, bars and restaurants.

## RESTAURANTS

The local speciality is thyme honey. Most restaurants are concentrated around the harbour:

### Cosar

One of the oldest establishments here. Traditional fish dishes. Very good value.
*Category 3*

### Liman

Restaurant with terrace much frequented by tourists.
*Category 2*

### Yunus

Tasty fish and seafood in a romantic atmosphere.
*Category 2*

## HOTELS

### Aktur Village

Bungalow village next to a large cove with pebble beach. Small restaurant.
*Aktur Tesisleri 607; Category 2; Tel. and Fax: 252/724 63 71*

### Club Maris

The Robinson Club complex has been here since April 1993. Comfortable and well-appointed. Even the drinks at the bar are included.

*400 rooms; Category 1; Tel: 252/436 92 00*

### Dorya Motel

Wonderful garden complex with 32 bungalow-apartments. Very well maintained.
*İskele Mah.; Category 2; Tel: 252/712 35 93*

### Mare Hotel

New three-star hotel with all mod. cons.
*50 rooms; Category 2; Tel: 252/712 32 11*

## SPORT & LEISURE

There are two other bathing beaches in Datça, apart from the ones attached to the Club Datça and Dorya Motel. But the best places for bathing are the coves off the beaten track. Boat trips are, therefore, in heavy demand. Skin diseases can apparently be cured in the 30°C heat of the thermal springs built by the Romans.

## ENTERTAINMENT

The best places to meet people and enjoy a drink in pleasant surroundings are the charming little bars down on the harbour.

## INFORMATION

### Turizm Danışma Bürosu

*Hükümet Binası; Tel: 252/712 31 63*

## SURROUNDING AREA

### Knidos                    (B5)

The remains of the acropolis here are worth seeing. The massive statue of Aphrodite by Praxiteles – the first female nude carved in marble and, in ancient times, one of the most famous sculptures in the world – has now sadly disappeared. The road to Knidos is not a good one and although there are dolmşues in summer, it's better to go there by boat. An added attraction is that the boats drop anchor in pretty bays along the way so that passengers may swim. *Daily departures from Datça harbour at 09.00 hrs, return around 19.00 hrs; Return trip approx. £6.50*

# FETHIYE

**(C5)** The district town of Fethiye (pop. 25000) lies on the ancient site of Telmessos and many of the boats in the harbour sail from here to the island of Kekova with its mysterious sunken cities. 🏃 Fethiye's souvenir shops, as well as its range of nightlife, restaurants and bars, make it a similar place to Bodrum.

If you need a rest from the overwhelming history and culture of Asia Minor, relax on the idyllic beach at Ölüdeniz (Dead Sea). This beautiful turquoise lagoon lies 12 km south of Fethiye. Nestling among pine covered mountains, it is always one of the first pictures shown in any guidebook to Turkey. It is strictly forbidden for yachts to cast anchor here. Other attractions include the Lycian rock tombs, dating from 400 BC. Two earthquakes struck the town in 1950 and 1957, but it was very quickly rebuilt.

## SIGHTS

### Lycian Rock Tombs
The tombs date from the 6th-4th centuries BC and are carved into a steep rock face above the town. The Lycians believed that winged demons, called Harpies, carried the dead to the heavens. Some of the tombs are copies of Greek temple façades, while others take the form of traditional Lycian houses. The ancient cult of the ancestor never produced as many necropoli as along this stretch of coast. The most beautiful tomb is that of Amyntas, a prominent Lycian of the 4th century BC.
*Behind the bus station*

## MUSEUM

### Fethiye Museum
Exhibits sarcophagi, marble heads and tomb reliefs from the excavations in Xanthos and the Letoön, as well as from the nearby Lycian sites of Pinara and Tlos.
*Daily (except Mon) 09.00-12.00 hrs and 13.30-17.30 hrs; 200 m outside town on the Akdeniz Cad.*

## RESTAURANTS

### Anfora
Traditionally designed restaurant. International and Turkish cuisine.
*Hamam Sok. 5 (opposite the Hamam); Category 1; Tel: 252/612 12 82*

### Güneş Restoran
The tables are arranged beneath an arcade of vines. Nice spot for lunch. Large selection of *mezeler*.
*Lykia Cad. (near the bazaar); Category 2; Tel: 252/614 27 76*

### Megri Restoran
Excellent Turkish dishes (especially the fish) at great prices.
*Haman Sok. (in the old town); Category 2; Tel: 252/614 40 46*

### Rafet
One of the best restaurants in town and very reasonably priced.

Recommended fish dish is *orfoz*, a type of perch.
*Kordonboyu; Category 2; Tel: 252/614 11 06*

### The White Dolphin

◁▷ This restaurant not only provides you with the best fish in town, but also offers one of the loveliest views of the Ölüdeniz beach. Great atmosphere at dusk.
*3 km outside Ölüdeniz; Category 2; Tel: 252/616 60 36*

There's a permanent fruit and vegetable market close to the Atatürk memorial. The carpet and souvenir shops are in the *Carsi Cad.*, parallel to the *Atatürk Cad.*

### Club Aldiana

Lovely holiday village with private cove and all mod. cons.
*360 rooms; Kalemya Koyu; Category 1; Tel: 252/614 83 60*

### Likya Hotel

The hotel is beautifully situated on the yacht marina.
*45 rooms; Karagözler Mah.; Category 2; Tel: 252/614 11 69*

### Meri Hotel

Pretty hotel at the end of the Ölüdeniz beach, with terraces

*The Amyntas Tomb was carved into the rock in Fethiye in 400 BC*

and a beautiful garden.
*75 rooms; Belcekiz; Category 2; Tel: 252/616 60 60*

## Robinson Club Lykia

Spacious complex with wonderfully designed buildings. Room for 1200 guests. Big, partly stony, beach. Excellent restaurant service. Has served as a location for films.
*15 km south of Fethiye; Category 1; Tel: 252/616 60 10 (Village), Tel: 252/616 64 10 (Residence)*

### SPORT & LEISURE

The main attraction here is the beautiful beach at Ölüdeniz. It costs around £2 to get on to the beach, but this fee includes the use of showers and toilets. For just £5 you can go on a day-long boat trip, which includes a picnic lunch, to the Sövalye isle or alternatively you can go on a round trip tour of the rocky coves or the 12 islands in the bay. (*Likya Tour Service at the harbour*).

The latest sporting attraction is paragliding from the surrounding hills directly on to the beach. A tandem-jump costs around £65. The prettiest cove, which can only be reached by sea, is Butterfly Bay, south of Ölüdeniz.

### ENTERTAINMENT

A trip on the boat-restaurant *Bonsoir Yüzen* out into the gulf is a very pleasant experience.
*Departure around 20.00 hrs; £13-17 including food and live music*

### INFORMATION

**Turizm Danışma Bürosu**
*Iskele Mey. 1; Tel: 252/614 15 27*

### SURROUNDING AREA

## Dalyan (B5)

A magical little holiday spot on the Dalyan river opposite the rock tombs of Kaunos. The fish restaurants on the river bank are first class and the hotels and pensions very comfortable. One of the main attractions is the 'Turtle beach' in the Dalyan delta, where sea turtles spawn. During the breeding period from June to September, the beach is barred to tourists from 18.00-09.00 hrs. The breeding areas are now under environmental protection.

60 km north-west of Fethiye, Dalyan is best reached by car. To get there, drive to Ortaca and then take the south-west fork to Dalyan. There is also a bus which takes you to Köyegiz, where boat trips are organized.

## Sarigerme (B-C5)

To get to the lovely sandy beach on the Bay of Sarigerme head due south from Ortaca.

# KUŞADASI

**(B4)** Kuşadası (pop. 22 000) is today one of the largest holiday resorts in Turkey. It lies in the middle of picturesque coastal scenery sprinkled with cypresses, olive trees and vines. It's a very popular holiday destination thanks to its close proximity to such extraordinary ancient sites as Aphrodisias, Ephesus, Milet, Didyma, Priene and Pamukkale. ✱ A wide variety of sporting activities is offered here, as well as excellent shopping, restaurants and an extremely lively nightlife. Kuşadası is also a well-known port of call for cruise-liners.

## SIGHTS

### Harbour

The old fishing harbour has been expanded into a modern marina with 600 berths. All types of boat moor here, from the Turkish *gulet* to the luxury yacht.

### Caravanserai

A stone's throw from the port, this former caravanserai, which has been converted into a hotel, is well worth a visit. The inner courtyards and gardens are splendid and it is a wonderful place to stop for tea.
*Atatürk Bul. 1*

## RESTAURANTS

### Ali Baba Fish Restaurant

One of the most expensive but best fish restaurants in the town.
*Town centre; Category 1*

### Camtepe

Beautifully presented Turkish specialities.
*Barbaros Hayrettin Bul.; Category 1*

## SHOPPING

Onyx, meerschaum pipes, jewllery, leather, carpets, copper and brass articles can all be found here. The best carpet store is the *Uner Carpet Gallery* on the harbour. Leather belts are good value at *Velider,* you can get quality leather clothes at *Kosar,* and good jewellery from *Opal,* opposite the post office.

## HOTELS

### Club Kervanseray

The former caravanserai of Öküz Mehmet Paşa is one of the most beautiful and original places to stay in Kuşadası.
*40 rooms; Atatürk Bul. 1; Category 1; Tel: 252/614 41 15*

### Club Méditerranée

Cool and casual club with a Turkish touch.
*478 rooms; Arslanburnu Mev.; Category 1; Tel: 252/614 11 35*

### Kismet

Situated on the Akyar peninsula, this hotel has a palm garden and a beautiful view of the bay.
*54 rooms; Akyar Mev.; Category 1; Tel: 252/614 20 05*

## SPORT & LEISURE

Kuşadası is an ideal place for surfing and sailing. Surfboards and sailing boats are available for hire from: *Turban Kuşadası Marina; Tel: 252/614 17 52*

Beaches: *Belediye Plajt* between the town centre and the yacht marina, and at the *Yilanci Burnu* promontory.

## ENTERTAINMENT

✝ The harbour area buzzes with nightlife. The top disco is the *Club Akdeniz, Karaova Mev.,* inside the hotel of the same name. Wild atmosphere.

## INFORMATION

### Turizm Danişma Bürosu

*İskele Mey.; Tel: 252/614 11 03*

## SURROUNDING AREA

### Aphrodisias                    (B4)

This site, dedicated to the Greek goddess of love, is one of the most fascinating places in Turkey.

*Aphrodisias has the best-preserved stadium of Antiquity*

◁▷ Against the backcloth of the Baba Dağı mountain, an almost completely intact white marble theatre lies nestling in a fairy-tale landscape. The small odeon, colossal remains of the Temple of Aphrodite, and the stadium – which could hold up to 30 000 spectators and is the largest and best-preserved in Turkey – can also be seen.

### Didyma (B4)

Didyma was once home to an oracle that rivalled the one at Delphi. According to legend, it was here where Alexander the Great learned that he would defeat the Persians. Had it been completed, the Temple of Apollo (some of which has been preserved) would have put even the Temple of Artemis at Ephesus in the shade. It is considered to be one of the Seven Wonders of the World, measures 110 x 50 m and rests on a seven-stepped base. It was originally surrounded by a portico of 120 double colonnades – three of the columns have been preserved. At the entrance to the temple is one of the huge heads of Medusa which once decorated a frieze on the facade. ◁▷ There is a panoramic view of the surrounding countryside from these impressive ruins.

### Railway Museum at Çamlik (B4)

Railway fans can trace the history of the Eastern railways from the restored original of the Baghdad train to some of the last steam locomotives made in America. Visitors can even climb aboard the well-preserved trains.
*18 km from Kuşadasi*

### Ephesus (B4

★ A walk through the ancient settlement of Ephesus is like taking a journey through time. The buildings, most of which date back to the Roman Empire between the 2nd and 4th centuries are still in good condition.

Before touring the sights of Ephesus, it is recommended that you visit the Archaeological Museum in *Selçuk* (pop. 19 000) • *Daily 08.30-16.30 hrs; 3 km from Ephesus*. Finds from Ephesus are displayed here, such as the cult statue of Artemis and the god of fertility, Priapos, with his oversized genitals. The ancient site can be reached from the museum on foot and the walk takes you past the remains of the Temple of Artemis, one of the Seven Wonders of the Ancient World.

Begin your tour of Ephesus at the Arcadian Way, a 530 m-long boulevard, once illuminated at night, which led from the old harbour (which has long since turned to sand) to the theatre at the end. Along the boulevard is the 200 x 240 m Verulanus Square and the Harbour Gym-

nasium with the partly uncovered baths. To the north lies the Church of St Mary, in which the ecumenical council established that Mary was the Mother of God (the origin of the cult of Mary) and thus put an end to the war of dogma with the patriarch of Constantinople.

The ancient Roman theatre is vast, with a capacity for 25 000 spectators. Despite some rather destructive 'restoration', it is still an impressive structure. Every

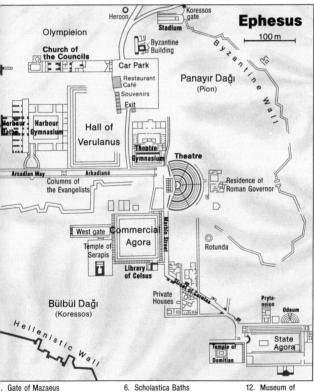

Ephesus

100 m

| Heroon | Koressos gate |
| Olympieion | Stadium |
| Church of the Councils | Byzantine Building |
| | Car Park |
| | Restaurant Café |
| | Souvenirs |
| | Exit |

Panayır Dağı (Pion)

Harbour Baths / Harbour Gymnasium

Hall of Verulanus

Arcadian Way / Arkadiané / Theatre Gymnasium / Theatre

Columns of the Evangelists

Residence of Roman Governor

West gate / Commercial Agora

Temple of Serapis

Rotunda

Library of Celsus

Private Houses

Street of Curetes

Prytaneion / Odeum

Bülbül Dağı (Koressos)

Hellenistic Wall

Temple of Domitian

State Agora

*The restored façade of the Library of Celsus at Ephesus*

January, it hosts the famous camel-wrestling competitions – *Dove Güresi* – a spectacle certainly worth seeing.

Once you have visited the theatre, make your way down Marble Street to the Library of Celsus. This building, which dates from the 2nd century, held 12 000 scrolls and was named after the governor of the province of Asia. The imposing façade has been painstakingly restored. There are many other interesting sites to see between the Upper and Lower Agora (see map on page 63). You should allow at least two hours for your visit here. *Entrance £2.50*

### Milet (B4)

The town is one of the oldest and was once one of the most powerful Greek cities of Asia Minor. It is a cradle of western thought – home to the philosopher Anaximenes (6th century BC), the mathematician Thales (625-545 BC) and the architect Hippodamus (5th century BC),

whose style can be seen in one o the earliest right-angled stree systems. In the 5th century BC Milet, or Miletus, was a peninsul in the Gulf of Latmos. The lan became bogged down in the sea sonal marshes of the Menderes and today the town finds itself further 8 km inland. The Baths o Faustina, said to have been estab lished by the wife of Marcus Au relius, are well-preserved, as is th Theatre, which has a capacity o 25 000 spectators.

### Pamukkale (B-C4

★ ↯ The 100m-high lime stone terraces at Pamukkal (which is Turkish for 'Cotto Castle') are the result of the accu mulation over thousands of year of salt deposits from the ho springs. This impressive plac shining a dazzling white in th sun, has become one of the sta attractions of a trip to Turke Unfortunately, though, the sit has begun to suffer from the hug amount of tourists, and some o the rocks have already turne lack. There have even been suggestions that the site might be closed, but it hasn't quite come to this yet. It's still possible to paddle about in the warm waters (about 5°C) on the terraces – but remember to remove your shoes.

If you want to float in blissful warmth, pay a visit to the Motel Pamukkale on top of the plateau. For a small fee, you can swim in the large pool above the remains of ancient columns, which date back to the time of the old spa town of Hierapolis. The water is said to be good for rheumatism and forms of gout. Below the terraces lies the village of Pamukkale, with its numerous cafés and restaurants.

## Priene (B4)

This ancient town was built, like Pergamon, on a rocky terrace. The streets and houses of Priene are of particular interest. The Greek architect Hippodamus laid the streets out like a chess board. Pointing in the direction of the four compass points, they each have right-angled junctions. The Temple of Athena is a masterpiece of Ionian architecture. ⚐ A trip to Priene is worth making just for the wonderful view of the Menderes valley and the surrounding mountains.

*All the above-listed sites around Kuşadası can be reached by bus or dolmuş.*

## MARMARIS

(B5) A good 30 years after an earthquake levelled it to the ground, Marmaris (pop. 16 000) and the surrounding area has developed into a thriving tourist centre – the third most popular

*The terraces of Pamukkale, known locally as 'Cotton Castle'*

resort in Turkey after Kuşadası and Bodrum. Nestling in the hollow of a wide, well-protected bay it is surrounded by pine trees and oleanders which is why it is often promoted as 'Green Marmaris'. The town is centred around a 16th century Ottoman castle where Suleiman the Magnificent amassed his troops for the battle against the Knights of St. John in Rhodes. One of the first prominent visitors to Marmaris was Lord Nelson, who took rest and shelter here in 1798 with the British fleet before sailing off to fight the French at the battle of Abukir (Egypt). Today, you'll see boats of every description bobbing up and down along the long, palm-fringed sea front. If you find the noise and congestion of Marmaris all a bit much, why not hire a boat with family or friends and take a trip along the Lycian coast. The captain will catch fresh fish for your supper and you sleep on deck under the stars. For many this is by far the loveliest and most relaxing way o spending a holiday in Turkey.

## SIGHTS

### Marmaris Marina
Stroll along the waterfront, from the heart of the old town to th new marina, and admire all th pleasure boats at anchor. Th promenade café is a particularl good spot for boat-watching.

### Marmaris Kalesi
Building work on the castle wa completed under Suleiman th Magnificent in 1522. It was re stored at great expense in 198 ☙ There's a beautiful view from the top of the castle over the bay
*Old town, above the yacht marina*

## RESTAURANTS

You'll find plenty of restauran on the promenade, but if yo want to escape the traffic nois look for a restaurant in one of th backstreets such as Yeni Kordon

*The Bay of Marmaris marks the dividing line between the Aegean and the Mediterranean*

**Yakamoz Restoran**

One of the best restuarants in Marmaris for fish and seafood.
Barbaros Cad.; Category 1; Tel: 252/412 51 60

**Gühal Restoran**

The speciality *keskek,* a stew made from chick-peas, chicken and spices is especially good.
Barbaros Cad. 23/A; Category 2

## SHOPPING

Marmaris has the most beautiful bazaar on the south coast, but the prices for souvenirs and luxury carpets are higher than average. Marmaris is famous for its varieties of honey, including thyme honey and virgin honey, which is the first honey from a new hive.

## HOTELS

**Altinyunus Hotel**

Spacious five-star complex with nightclub, casino and fitness centre. Service is perfect.
264 rooms; Pamucak Mev. 48700; Category 1; Tel: 252/412 36 17

**Lydia Hotel**

The oldest and one of the most charming hotels boasts a lovely palm beach and flower garden.
333 rooms; Siteler; Category 2; Tel: 252/412 29 40

**Yavuz Hotel**

Decorated in the Ottoman style with its own confectioner's shop.
51 rooms; Atatürk Cad. 58; Category 2; Tel 252/412 29 37

## SPORT & LEISURE

There are facilities for almost every type of watersport in the Bay of Marmaris. ★ If you want to go on a cruise, the cheapest yacht charters start at around £90 per person per day. These should be booked through travel agents, or else by going directly to the yacht skippers in the marina. The nicest beaches lie towards Içmeler, about 7 km from Marmaris. There are organized boat excursions to the surrounding islands and beaches.

## ENTERTAINMENT

🏃 The best places to go dancing are the Disco Maxim in the Atatürk Cad. and the Turban Disco in the holiday village of the same name, on the road to Içmeler. The dance floor here extends right out to the sea. Otherwise, you'll find plenty of nightlife in the harbour area.

## INFORMATION

**Turizm Danişma Bürosu**
İskele Mey. 39; Tel: 252/412 10 35

## SURROUNDING AREA

**Bozburun** (B5)
In the last few years, this village (pop. 1200) has become a boom town for yacht skippers. It has many restaurants, bars and shops. Inland, you find villages almost entirely unspoilt by tourism. You'll be hard pressed to find any real sandy beaches along the jagged, fjord-like bay of Bozburun, but right on the seashore is a real gem – Sabrina's Guesthouse. It is an oriental-style country house with comfortable rooms and delightful Turkish food.
7 rooms; Category 2; Tel: 252/456 20 45, Fax: 456 24 70

# The Turkish riviera

*The 'White Sea' and rugged Taurus mountains provided the dramatic setting for the romance of Antony and Cleopatra*

Protected by the Taurus Mountains to the north, the coastal region stretching from Fethiye to Alanya covers the territory of the ancient provinces of Lycia and Pamphylia and is scattered with ruins from Greek and Roman times. Here too are the legendary Lycian rock tombs, hewn into the face of the rugged and imposing cliffs. The modern coast road provides easy access to all these historical treasures. The climate makes this area a holidaymaker's paradise – the locals claim that you can bathe in the Akdeniz, or 'White Sea', practically all year round from early spring until well into autumn – with ideal conditions prevailing during the periods that fall on either side of the high season. The shelter afforded by the 4000 m-high Taurus range has given rise to rich vegetation. Despite high temperatures and low rainfall, the conditions are perfect for the cultivation of lemons, bananas, avocados and olives which grow in abundance. Rocky coves and outcrops alternate with long sandy beaches. It comes as no surprise, therefore, that more than half of Turkey's tourist accommodation is concentrated along this 400 km strip of coast. Although some parts have been ruined by large-scale, haphazard hotel building, there remain many unspoilt spots and undiscovered villages where the locals provide a warm and friendly welcome. Besides the excellent watersports along the coast, the region provides beautiful mountain scenery where you can walk for miles without seeing another soul.

## ALANYA

(**D4**) ★ Situated at the foot of the Taurus amid orange and lemon groves, this town of 52 000 inhabitants has the oldest tourist tradition on the south coast. It started to cater for mass tourism as far back as the 1960s, sacrificing many old buildings for new hotels, and the old town retreated back to its original site up on the castle hill. The castle was built in

*Visible for miles, the rock tombs at Kale are the finest on the Lycian coast*

69

1221 AD by the Seljuk sultan Aladdin Keykubat I, who chose Alanya as his winter residence. The castle is still well-preserved. Around 1000 years earlier, Mark Antony had presented the town and the whole of Cilicia to Cleopatra, who used the rich local cedar forests for ship-building material. Alanya is known today by the Turks as 'Little Germany' because of the huge numbers of German tourists who come here year after year.

## SIGHTS

### Arap Evliyesi
This imposing 13th century Seljuk citadel comprises three fortresses, built one within the next, and boasts no less than 146 towers. Inside the uppermost citadel (*İç Kale*) is the Byzantine chapel dedicated to St George, and beneath the outcrop are the walls of the Ehmedek Castle. ⮟⮝ From the cliff-top citadel, you get a wonderful view of the town, the bay and the sea. The castle is situated on the Kale hill and is accessible by road.

### Damlatas Caves
Underground stalactite cave with a high level of humidity, said to benefit asthma and rheumatism sufferers.
*Entrance: 200 metres behind the tourist office, Carsi Mah.*

### Cave Tour
At the foot of the castle rock are a number of caves which can only be reached by boat, amongst which are the 'Lovers' Cave', the 'Phosphorous Cave' and the 'Pirates Cave'. The castle is believed to have been linked to the beach via an underground passage, and legend has it that Cleopatra used this tunnel when she wanted to go swimming.
*The boat trip lasts 1 hr, costs around £2.00 and starts from the harbour*

### Kızıl Kule (Red Tower)
The octagonal, 33 m-high tower is the principal landmark on the harbour. It was built between 1224 and 1228 AD, and later renovated in 1951. There is an ethnographic museum on the ground floor: *open daily (except Mon) 09.00-12.00 and 13.30-17.30 hrs*

### Tersane (Shipyard)
The shipyard was hewn out of the cliff face in 1227 AD and its 40 m-deep workshops open to the sea. A medium sized fleet could shelter here from enemy vessels. Tersane was considered to be the safest base on the south coast and small ships are still built here today. There are organized boat trips to the workshops.
*Departure from the harbour*

## MUSEUM

### Alanya Müzesi (Alanya Museum)
Archaeological exhibits, coins, ceramics and carpets.
*Daily (except Mon) 09.00-12.00 and 13.30-17.00 hrs; Entrance approx. 90p*

## RESTAURANTS

### Mahperi Sultan Restoran
The best and most expensive restaurant in Alanya.
*Gazi Paşa Cad.; Category 1*

### Yönet Restoran
Fish restaurant with terrace and view of the harbour.

*The imposing Seljuk fortress at Alanya overlooking the town and the sea*

Keykubat Cad.; Category 2; Tel: 242/513 30 96

## SHOPPING

You will find a number of souvenir shops around the port trading in gold and silver jewellery, kilims, hand-painted calabashes, etc. But Alanya is above all renowned for its silk weaving and the local tradition of silkworm breeding dates back to the 6th century. *Bürümcük,* or silk, is the ideal summer fabric and can be bought cheaply in the bazaar district, where the shopper faces an agonizing choice of colours and patterns. There's a tailor in the *İskele Cad. 15* who makes clothes to measure at very reasonable prices.

## HOTELS

**Azak Hotel**
Small, high-quality hotel with ornate architecture. Swimming pool.

# MARCO POLO SELECTION: WESTERN MEDITERRANEAN

**1 Alanya**
Alanya is renowned for its fine silk, the perfect fabric for the summer heat
(page 69)

**2 Antalya**
This picturesque Ottoman town was once described by Atatürk as 'the most beautiful town in the world'
(page 73)

**3 Diving**
Kas and the Kekova region are a diver's paradise
(page 76)

**4 Side**
To watch a spectacular sunset over the sea, the best seats in the house are the upper tiers of the ancient theatre at Side
(page 78)

*51 rooms; Saray Mah.; Category 2; Tel: 242/513 91 55*

### Club Alantur

A large-scale complex that can accommodate 800 people, but there is plenty of room for them all on the beach.

*318 rooms; Dimcayi Mev.; Category 1; Tel: 242/513 44 16*

### Grand Hotel Atilla

Small hotel with two swimming pools. Each room has its own balcony.

*61 rooms; Oba Köyü Göl Mev.; Category 2; Tel: 242/513 09 35*

### Hamdullah Paşa Turistik Tesisleri

Exclusive holiday complex by the sea accommodating up to 1100 guests.

*308 suites; 8 km outside town; Category 1; Tel: 242/565 15 20*

**SPORT & LEISURE**

Situated to the west of the castle, Alanya has a lovely long sandy beach that stretches for a few kilometres.

**ENTERTAINMENT**

The nightlife here is nothing to get too excited about, but the best discos are the *Banana, on the beach of the Hotel Banana in the Cikcili Köyü; Tel: 242/511 15 48* and the *Panel Disco, also on the beach, 2 km beyond the Banana.*

**INFORMATION**

**Turizm Danişma Bürosu**
*Carsi Mah.; Tel: 242/513 12 40*

**SURROUNDING AREA**

### Dim Çay                              (D4

An alternative to the sand and salt water of the beach is a trip to the magical valley and cool clear waters of the River Dim. This is a little oasis in the heart of the mountains. The banks of the river are lined with restaurant and snack-bars selling fresh fish or kebabs and the river is straddled by a picturesque suspension bridge. To get to Dim Çay, take the E24 eastwards from Alanya and turn left after about 8 km.

*The historic backdrop to the beach at Alanya*

# ANTALYA

(C4) Antalya's claim to be the jewel of the Turkish Riviera is well-founded. The town (pop. 614 000) stands majestically on top of a rocky plateau, where the developers have managed to pull off the rare feat of erecting new hotels while still retaining the old town charm. Wide boulevards lead into the historic centre which is laced with a maze of narrow streets, where traders and artisans go about their business, and an assortment of Seljuk buildings from the Middle Ages, all of which lend the place its special eastern charm. Beyond the avenues lined with palms, plane trees and oleander, the fertile plain of Pamphylia stretches as far as the snow-covered slopes of the Taurus mountains. The harbour of Antalya is one of the prettiest on the Mediterranean coast. The basin is enclosed by ancient but solid and imposing quay walls, on top of which stands a clutch of restaurants and cafés. The renovation of the old town has, in fact, been recognized with an award.

## SIGHTS

### Old Town

★ A walk through the little lanes of the old town between *Cumhuriyet Cad.* and *Atatürk Cad.* soon makes you realize why Kemal Atatürk once described Antalya as the 'most beautiful town in the world'. The key places of interest are in the Kaleiçi district around the Clock Tower, known as the *Saat Kule.* The official symbol of the town is the *Yivli Minare,* or 'Fluted Minaret', built in 1220 with pink bricks. Behind it stands the *Alaeddin Cami,* a six-domed mosque built in 1373, which was originally a Byzantine basilica. Hadrian's Gate, built in 130 AD, leads via a stairway adorned with Corinthian columns to the old quarter. Beyond the Atatürk Memorial, a flight of steps leads to the harbour.

❧ The Mermeli Teagarden offers the best view of the tastefully renovated old harbour and can be reached via the steps by the harbour mole.

## MUSEUM

### Antalya Arkeoloji Müzesi (Archaeological Museum)

The museum has an important collection of antiquities, including many statues from Perge, and finds from Aspendos and Kekova dating back to Greco-Roman times, as well as relics of St Nicholas from Demre, or Kale as it is known today.
*Kenan Evren Cad.; open daily (except Mon) 08.00-12.00 and 13.30-17.00 hrs*

## RESTAURANTS

Prices in the restaurants along the harbour tend to be expensive, but on the *Sebziciler Içi Sok.*, close to the bazaar and parallel with Atatürk Cad., is a covered passageway with plenty of cheaper local restaurants.

### Ahtapot

Excellent sea-food.
*Kaleici, by the marina; Category 2*

### Blue Parrot Café

Quality international cuisine in the heart of the old town. Tables are set in a garden planted with

orange trees.
*İzmirli Ali Efendi Sok. 10; Category 1; Tel: 242/247 03 49*

## Club 29

Romantic restaurant with a wonderful view of the harbour and dinners by candlelight.
*Kaleici, by the marina; Category 1; Tel: 242/241 62 60*

## Marina

Nouvelle cuisine is a speciality in the gourmet restaurant of the Marina Hotel. The restaurant is situated in the beautiful inner courtyard.
*Mermerli Sok. 15; Category 1; Tel: 242/247 54 90*

## Yedi Mehmet

❂ This restaurant is frequented predominantly by businessmen and their families.
*Konyaalti Beach; Category 2; Tel: 242/241 16 41*

SHOPPING

Stores selling leather goods, and fashion boutiques, are centred around the *Yivli Minare*, while gold and silver jewellery can be found in the *Atatürk Cad.* In the *İskele Cad.*, a small sidestreet in the old town, you'll find numerous other souvenir shops selling carpets and copperware. If you're looking for chic, then go to the boutiques along the palm-lined *Atatürk Bul.*

HOTELS

## Antares Hotel

Small, charming hotel with intimate atmosphere.
*38 rooms; Lara Cad. 1537; Category 2; Tel: 242/223 22 44*

## Aspen Hotel

Comfortable hotel in the old town.
*40 rooms; Kaledibi Sok. 16; Category 2; Tel: 242/247 71 78*

## Marina

An old Turkish architectural delight restored with love and taste.
*42 rooms; Kaleici, Memerli Sok. 15; Category 1; Tel: 242/247 54 90*

## Yalcin Hotel

Basic hotel in the town centre.
*32 rooms; Hüsnü Karakas Cad.; Category 3; Tel: 242/241 89 32*

SPORT & LEISURE

There are two fine beaches here – the Konyaalti that extends from the harbour to the eastern edge of the town and the Lara, 9 km east of Antalya, where the larger package holiday hotels are situated. Dolmuşes run there every 15 minutes. As well as watersports on the coast, there are ski facilities around Saklikent. In the late spring you can combine skiing in the morning with an afternoon swim in the Mediterranean. Daily excursions to the mountains 25 km away are organized by the *Akay tourist office, Cumhuriyet Cad. 47; Tel: 242/241 27 47*

ENTERTAINMENT

✱ Nightlife is centred around the many cafés and clubs along the harbour. ❧ The garden of the *Club 29* restaurant has an open air dancefloor and bar overlooking the sea. The surroundings of the Konyaalti Strand are less elegant, but it's a good place if you're in the mood for something a little more lively. For something more traditional, belly dancing is performed regularly at the Hotel Talya (*Fevzi Cakmak Cad.; Weds and Sun*)

## INFORMATION

**Turizm Danişma Bürosu**
*Cumhuriyet Cad. 91; Tel: 242/241 17 47; Daily 09.00-18.00 hrs*

## SURROUNDING AREA

### Aspendos                                    (D4)
This Roman theatre with a capacity for 20000 spectators was built in the 2nd century AD during the reign of Marcus Aurelius. It is one of the finest of its kind and well worth a visit. In Seljuk times, the theatre served as a stopover for caravan travellers. The acoustics are amazing and the theatre is so well-preserved that 1800 years on, concerts, plays, and even grease-wrestling tournaments are still staged here.

### Düden Waterfalls                           (D4)
❖ A large picnic site has been built by the upper falls, from where you can appreciate the full force of the thundering cascades. The entrance is via a gap in the rock which passes under the main waterfall itself. The lower waterfalls, situated on the road to Lara beach, drop about 60 m down into the sea. You can climb up to see them in a dolmuş or else take a boat from the harbour in Antalya (*departures three times daily*) and see them from below.

### Kemer                                      (C4)
This former fishing port has been tastefully transformed into a first class tourist resort complete with marina, luxury hotels, shops and discotheques, as well as some excellent holiday villages – Club Aldiana Milta, two Club Méditerranée resorts and the Robinson Club Camyuva, whose attractive Ottoman and Byzantine-style bungalows contrast starkly with the skyscraper hotels found in less well-designed resorts. The rocky coast and offshore islands are a diver's paradise.
*40 km south west of Antalya*

### Olympos                                    (C4)
The ruins of the port of Olympos, built in the 3rd century BC, lie in a beautiful forest and are overgrown in places by trees and shrubs. Among other things, you can see the remains of a giant temple gate and a theatre. It's about an hour on foot from here to Yanartas, a rocky mound where dozens of flames burn incessantly. Natural methane is at the source of this eternal fire, but according to legend the flames were emitted by the fire-breathing monster, Chimaera, slain by Bellerophon.
*Turn right off the main road between Finike and Kemer*

### Perge                                      (D4)
Impressive ruins reveal how mighty this ancient Pamphylian city must once have been. You can still see a theatre, baths, a stadium, an acropolis, colonnaded streets and city gates. Visitors should allow themselves plenty of time to look at the interesting details of the friezes and statues.
*Dolmuşes from Antalya*

### Termessos                                  (C4)
The natural defences of this ancient ruined city perched high up

in the Taurus mountains enabled it to remain one of the few in Asia Minor not to be conquered by Alexander the Great. There are the remains of a gymnasium, several temples and a necropolis, whose sarcophagi lie strewn about as a result of numerous earthquakes. ꕔ The best-preserved building is the open-air theatre directly above the gorge, which provides a wonderful view across the Antalya plain. Termessos lies within one of the most beautiful national parks in Turkey; the Güllük Daği (1050 m). There is also a small museum. *Daily (except Mon) 08.30-17.00 hrs.*

# KAŞ

(C5) The town (pop. 4500), which was built on the ruins of the ancient Antiphellos, has been transformed into a major tourist centre – and this within only a few years since the arrival of the first backpackers. The climate favours the growth of rubber plants, citrus fruits, palms and, most recently, hotels. Kaş is also the departure point for boat excursions to the nearby ancient underwater cities around the island of Kekova. Excursions are also available to the fishing village of Kale, which is renowned for its necropolis with Lycian tombs.

**Antiphellos**
There are few traces left of the ancient Lycian town of Antiphellos. There are a a number of sarcophagi, among them one Lycian tomb dating from the 4th century BC, and near the port, 2km from the city centre, ꕔ there is a Hellenistic theatre, hewn from natural stone, which offers a lovely view of the sea.

The restaurants between the harbour and the bus station load their counters in the evening with a wide range of tempting and inexpensive specialities. One of the best places is the Eris Restoran (*Cumhuriyet Mey.; Tel: 242/886 10 57*) where the atmosphere is relaxed. Kebabs and *köfte* are on offer at the Eva Kent restaurant (*by the bus station*).

**Aqua-Park**
The best hotel in town with a swimming pool overlooking the sea. Glass-bottomed boats can be hired for moonlight trips to Kekova.
*106 rooms; Category 1; Tel: 242/836 19 01*

**Medusa Hotel**
Pretty roof-terrace. All rooms with shower, some with balcony.
*23 rooms; Küciikcakil Mev.; Category 2; Tel: 242/836 14 40*

★ Kaş and the island of Kekova offer ideal conditions for diving – the water is warm, clear and teeming with fish. As well as the wildlife, you will also discover the ruins of an ancient city and a Byzantine basilica beneath the surface. Unaccompanied diving is not permitted, but the Hotel Likya (*Tel: 242/836 12 70*) has a diving school with English-speaking instructors.

**Turizm Danişma Bürosu**
*Cumhuriyet Mey. 6; Tel: 242/836 12 38*

## SURROUNDING AREA

### Kale (Demre) (C5)
Kale is the official name of Demre, known as Myra in Antiquity. It became the capital of Lycia in the 5th century AD. In the early Middle Ages, the basilica of St Nicholas, Bishop of Myra, became a place of pilgrimage, but visitors today are drawn here to see the ancient necropolis (*Daily 09.00-17.30 hrs; Entrance approx. 40p*). The rock tombs here, some of which are carved with beautiful reliefs, are the finest in Lycia. There is also a well-preserved Roman theatre.

### Kalkan (C5)
✪ Kalkan is a sleepy little town, though with the construction of the modern yacht marina it is gradually gearing itself towards tourism. Picturesque little side-streets, the old fishermen's houses, and the pebble-beached cove all add to its charm. There are a number of small pensions, such as Akin (*Atatürk Cad.; Category 3; Tel: 242/886 10 25*) as well as larger hotels such as the 3-star Hotel Pirat (*Kalkan Marinasi; Category 2; Tel: 242/886 11 78*). Excursions to the Ölüdeniz beach or donkey-trekking into the mountains, are organized by Armes Travel (*Yat Limani; Tel: 242/886 11 69*). The coast road between Kalkan and Kaş is one of the most beautiful drives you can take in the whole of Turkey, as it affords some spectacular views of the easternmost point of Greece, the Meyisti islands.

### Patara (C5)
Patara, the birthplace of St Nicholas (280-342 AD), had its heyday in Roman times when it served as a supply base for the army and as residence for the Roman governor. Later, Patara was to share the fate of many ports in Asia Minor — it became silted up. The remains of the giant Hadrian's granary, a triumphal arch, theatre and baths can still be seen. Patara's main attraction, however, is its stunning, 8 km-long and 400 m-wide beach, where the sand is almost pure white, burning hot in the summer, and the water is crystal clear. Beware, however, of strong prevailing currents.

### Xanthos (C5)
The town was the capital of Lycia before Myra and had as its motto 'better dead than enslaved'. Its inhabitants were renowned for their courage and pride, twice destroying their own city, and everyone in it, in order to evade capture. The relics of Lycian culture are very impressive, and include the Harpy pillar, a Roman theatre and the Nereid Monument – a beautiful Ionic temple, many of whose friezes are now housed in the British Museum.

## SIDE

(D4) Side was already inhabited by the 13th century BC and was Pamphylia's most important commercial port. It was for a long time a prosperous town. Its people profited from the lucrative slave trade until 67 BC — Egyptian records reveal that Side's main slave commodities were Black Africans and Nubians (from southern Egypt and present day Sudan). It reached its prosperous peak when it was under Roman rule, but the city fell into decline as the Roman Empire collapsed. Burnt to the ground and invaded by Arabs, Side was gradually abandoned and by the 12th century it had become a ghost town. Then in 1898 the arrival of Muslim Turk immigrants from Crete gave the town a new lease of life. But Side's new era of prosperity came in the 1960s, when the tourist boom began .

This small town has a romantic charm all of its own. It is like an open-air museum, where the numerous hotels, restaurants and cafés sit huddled among picturesque ancient ruins and historic buildings. Although access is forbidden to cars, Side gets completely overrun with people in the height of summer and those seeking peace and quiet should come in the spring or late autumn.

SIGHTS

### Ancient Buildings

A colonnaded street leads through the Monumental Gate to the Agora, where slave traders once held auctions. Today, the same spot accommodates a covered market hall, behind which stands the theatre. ★ This impressive structure (2nd century AD) with a capacity for 15 000 spectators, is the largest theatre in Pamphylia, towering above all the other ruins in Side. ⋈ At sunset there is a marvellous view from the upper tiers, but unfortunately the building has been temporarily closed to visitors while repair work is carried out.

MUSEUM

### Arkeoloji Müzesi (Archaeological Museum)

The museum is housed in the former Roman baths and their splendid gardens. The building has been beautifully restored, to reveal the *apodyterium* (cloakroom), *calidarium* (hot room),

*The theatre of Side is a perfect place to watch the sun set*

*sudarium* (steam room) and *frigidarium* (cold room). Exhibits include a collection of statues of the gods, jewellery, amphorae and several sarcophagi. The museum's greatest treasure is undoubtedly the statue of the Three Graces.
*Daily (except Mon) 08.30-11.30 and 13.00-17.00 hrs; Entrance approx. £3; Opposite the Agora*

## RESTAURANTS

Though there are many restaurants on the harbour and in the 'colonnaded street' few can really be recommended. The restaurants on the corniche above the town are more expensive, but they are in more pleasant surroundings. *Soundwave* is one of the most expensive, but the food is very good. The *Suppen Shop* in the old marketplace, which is open almost 24 hours a day, serves good food at reasonable prices.

## SHOPPING

Jewellery, leather and carpet shops are in plentiful supply along the colonnaded street. Jewellery is especially good value here, and you can usually rely on it being genuine, but the price you ultimately pay will always depend on your bargaining skills.

## HOTELS

There is a wide choice of hotels (although most are fully booked in summer) alongside many small pensions.

### Asteria Hotel
The most beautiful and luxurious hotel currently available in Side.

*310 rooms; Category 1; Tel: 242/753 18 30*

### Kleopatra Hotel
Small inexpensive family hotel. All rooms are fitted with a shower.
*40 rooms; Category 2; Tel: 242/753 10 33*

## SPORT & LEISURE

All the beaches are freely accessible, offering a wide range of activities from surfing to parascending.

## ENTERTAINMENT

There are numerous all-night discos here – one of the best is *Nimfeon*, on the way to the beach.

## INFORMATION

**Turizm Danışma Bürosu**
*Side Yolu Üzeri; Tel: 242/753 12 65*

## SURROUNDING AREA

### Manavgat Waterfalls            (D4)
❖ The waterfalls of the Manavgat river, which flows down from the Taurus mountains, are about 8 km from Side. Unwind over a cup of *çay* or sample the delicious trout and char-grilled chicken in one of the restaurants below the falls. From the restaurant terraces, you can watch brave people jumping into the falls. Two holiday complexes recommended in Manavgat are: Club Ali Bey (*436 rooms; Kazilagac Köyü, Manavgat; Category 1; Tel: 242/742 22 00*) a tiled palace, straight out of 'The Arabian Nights'; while the Robinson Club Pamfilya (*400 rooms; Manavgat; Category 1; Tel: 242/756 93 50*) is the perfect dream holiday destination.

# On the trail of the crusaders

*Inviting yet forbidding – Turkey's deep south is shrouded in myth and breathtaking natural beauty*

The eastern Mediterranean coast is an area of stark contrasts and great natural beauty. The 670 km stretch of coast, from the east of Alanya to Antakya on the Syrian border, was called Cilicia by the Romans. It can be sub-divided into three main geographical areas. The mountainous area from Antalya to Silifke was referred to by the Romans as Cilicia Tracheia or 'Rough Cilicia' because of the harsh but breathtaking landscape. The steep slopes of the Taurus mountains plummet down to the sea, punctuating the white, sandy beaches below. Eastward, beyond Mersin, the Cilician Plain begins. This marshy basin, with its fields of cotton, is one of the most fertile and richest regions in Turkey and was referred to by the Romans as Cilicia Campestris or 'Gentle Cilicia'. The area east of Adana, as far as Hatay, is the border province of Syria, the capital of which is Antakya.

*The island castle of Kızkalesi is shrouded in legend*

The history of Cilicia is one of conquests, fierce battles and piracy. The area's most notorious inhabitants were its pirates, until general Pompey wiped them out in 67 BC for plundering Roman ships. Old Phoenician settlements are dotted between castles built by the Crusaders; village girls go to pay homage to Priapos, the god of fertility; and tourists go to see the Maiden Bath, or Kizlar Hamami; wander through 'Heaven and Hell' and visit the first Christian church; or the battlefield of Issos, where Alexander the Great delivered his crushing defeat over the Persian king Darius III in 333 BC. The quiet beaches here are a secondary attraction for tourists, who come primarily to explore the historic sites and ancient ruins, and admire the majestic mountains and wild coastal landscape.

## ADANA

**(F3)** With its three-laned boulevards and elegant shops, Adana (pop. 1.2 million) is the image of

81

a bustling metropolis. The array of jewellers and goldsmiths with their lavish window displays is dazzling and explains why Adana is known as the 'city of gold', even though the most important industry is actually textiles. Adana is the fourth largest city in Turkey and is a place of many contrasts, embracing European and Eastern, rural and urban, old and modern, rich and poor. The richest industrialists and farmers in Turkey come from Adana.

## SIGHTS

### Taş Köprü
The 16 arches of Hadrian's stone bridge have spanned the river Seyhan for the last 1800 years and traffic still rolls across it today.

### Ulu Camii
Syrian influence is evident in the architecture of this mosque, built in 1541 – the tiles from İznik and Kütahya which decorate the interior are well worth seeing.
*Kizilay Cad.*

## MUSEUMS

### Adana Bölge Müzesi (Adana Regional Museum)
The museum houses a valuable collection of utensils, coins, jewellery, sculptures and sarcophagi from ancient Greek, Roman and Byzantine times.
*Daily (except Mon) 09.00-17.30 hrs; Next to the bus station*

### Atatürk Müzesi (Atatürk Museum)
Atatürk lived in this house during his sojourns in Adana and the exhibits, ranging from his nightcap to his newspaper, illustrate the more habitual concerns of his

daily life. There are also two gold-painted plaster busts of Atatürk on display.
*Daily 09.00-12.00 and 13.30-17.30 hrs; İnönü Cad.*

## RESTAURANTS

Because of the strong Arabic influence in this area, the food is generally spicier around here. The best-known local speciality is the spicy *Adana Kebab. Aslama,* a drink made from liquorice, is sold by street vendors in the summer, while *salgam suyu,* made from beetroot and carrot juice, is a popular drink in the winter. Among the best restaurants are the *Liman Lokantasi* and the *Onbasilar.* (*Both on the Atatürk Cad. opposite the tourist office*)

## SHOPPING

Gold and silver jewellery is relatively cheap and can be bought both at the bazaar and in shops.

## HOTEL

### Büyük Sürmeli Oteli
Luxury hotel with excellent restaurant (Arabic specialities).
*166 rooms; Ozler Cad.; Category 1; Tel: 322/452 36 00*

## ENTERTAINMENT

If you don't feel like dancing yourself, you can always be entertained by the mermerising belly-dancers who perform in many of the nightclubs.

## INFORMATION

### Turizm Danişma Bürosu
*Atatürk Cad. 13; Tel: 322/359 19 94*

### SURROUNDING AREA

**Silifke** **(E4)**

Although you probably won't wish to spend an extended period of time here, the town of Silifke (pop. 30 000) is well worth a visit. The Silifke Castle was built in the 3rd century BC and from the time of the Crusaders to the late Middle Ages provided an important strategic defence. King Barbarossa drowned in the River Göksu, which runs through the centre of the town, in an attack on Silifke in 1190, during the Third Crusade. The remains of the castle on the western edge of the town date back to the Middle Ages. If you climb up to the hill on foot, you'll pass an impressive cistern on the way. ◁▷ There's a superb view of the town, the plain and the Taurus. The main attraction in the Silifke Museum is the collection of coins dating

*The Cilician Gate was for centuries the only route from Tarsus to the Anatolian plateau*

back to Alexander the Great, discovered in 1980. Also on display are some Roman sculptures and folkloric items.

*Daily (except Mon) 09.00-12.30 and 13.30-17.30 hrs; Taşucu Yolu*

### Tarsus and the Cilician Gate (Gülek Boğazi) (F3)

Tarsus (pop. 180 000) has a documented history of 3000 years. St Paul was born here and Antony and Cleopatra fell in love here. The queen is also said to have ridden through the Cleopatra Gate, on the Mersin Cad., in 41 BC. This aside, the town has little historical interest and remains primarily an industrial centre.

It's worth making the 50 km trip northwards from Tarsus to see the Cilician Gate, a fearsome mountain gorge which for a long time was the only way to cross the Taurus mountains – for Alexander the Great as well as the troops in the First World War.

## ANAMUR

(E4) Although this town (pop. 37 000) is pleasantly situated, it has very little worth seeing, but provides a good base from which to visit the surrounding sites. The town that you see today started to develop in the 1950s and despite its long beaches, Anamur doesn't really feature on the tourist's map. Many local farmers make a living growing bananas here.

★ The road from Alanya to Anamur offers some splendid scenery.

### RESTAURANTS

A speciality in Anamur is the nomadic dish *yörük yemegli*, very thin flat bread with a variety of fillings. The nicest place to sit, eat and drink is in Anamur's little harbour, İskele. The restaurants here are all fairly cheap and serve good food. You may find that the choice is limited, but fish and kebabs are always in plentiful supply.

### SHOPPING

There's a wide choice of kilims featuring traditional nomadic animal motifs on sale in the bazaar district.

### HOTELS

Almost all the hotels are in Anamur's harbour, İskele.

### Eser Pansiyonu

Small, warm and friendly hotel with a roof terrace, a garden and very good food.

*İskele Makallesi; Category 3; Tel: 324/814 23 22*

### Hermes Hotel

Modern, mid-range hotel with good service and many extras.

*70 rooms; İskele Vivari Mev.; Category 2; Tel: 324/814 40 45*

### INFORMATION

### Turizm Danişma Bürosu

*Atatürk Bul. 64; Daily 08.00-18.00 hrs; Tel: 324/814 35 29*

### SURROUNDING AREA

### Anamur Kalesi (Anamur Castle) (E4)

★ ⩗ The castle stands proud and defiant as it watches over the southern tip of Asia Minor, the Cape of Anamur. It's an impressive structure and has been very

*The castle fortifications at Anamur have repelled many enemies into the sea*

well preserved. Built by the king of Armenia in the 12th century, the castle serves as a reminder of the time when pirates made the seas a treacherous place, causing havoc amongst the Crusaders on their long journey to the Holy Land. The mosque, baths and the pump room were all added during the expansion of the castle under the Ottomans.

*6 km from Anamur by dolmuş or by bus*

## Cennet ve Cehennem (E4)

★ The Caves of Heaven and Hell are among the most impressive of the limestone caverns scattered along the coast. The Cave of Heaven is in fact a 250 m-long and 70 m-deep gorge, entered via steps cut into the rock. At the bottom of the gorge is the Cave of Typhon, named after the mythological fire-breathing lizard and father of Cerberus, the three-headed dog who guarded the entrance to Hades. As you descend, the air becomes progressively

more difficult to breathe and a muffled rumbling can be heard – this is produced by an underground stream once thought to be the Styx. Although this may seem like Hades, the real Hell is the climb back up! At the entrance to the cave is the Byzantine and eerily beautiful Chapel of the Virgin Mary, built in the 5th century AD. The Cave of Hell itself is accessible only to potholers and was believed to be another entrance to Hades.

## Kızkalesi (E4)

The island fortress of Kızkalesi (Maiden's Castle) stands in the sea, 200 m from the beach. Its white walls rising out of the blue water create an impressive scene. According to legend, the castle was built by a sultan after he had been told by an oracle that his daughter would be killed by a snake, and he thought a castle in the water would provide the best protection. The snake, however, found its way into the castle in a basket and fulfilled the oracle's prophecy. You can either swim out to the castle, or else take a boat. The resort of Kizkalesi has a wonderful sandy beach which gets very crowded in summer, but the small town also makes a good base for touring the area and walking in the mountains.

## Narlikuyu                      (E4)
You only have to pay a small charge to visit the 4th century Maiden Bath, or *Kizlar Hamami*. In the bathhouse is a beautiful mosaic depicting the Three Graces and daughters of Zeus – Aglaia, Euphrosyne and Thalia. Close to the site are a number of lovely fish restaurants.

## ANTAKYA

**(F4)** A walk through the labyrinthine streets of the old town calls to mind the history of what was formerly Antioch. At one time Greek, Antioch gradually evolved into an Arabian town over the centuries, later becoming Turkish. In its heyday, Antioch was the third most important town in the ancient world after Alexandria and Rome, with a population of over 500 000. Later, it became the centre of early Christianity and the nucleus of

the Catholic Church – both Peter and Paul worked here. The population is of mixed origin, as is the case in the entire province of Hatay, with Turkish and Arabic vying with each other to be recognized as the main language.

Despite the many interesting sights in the town, Antakya isn't a tourist resort. The town suffered some devastating damage from earthquakes and was plundered many times, thus leading to its decline. But even though its glory days are gone, the charm of the town remains.

## SIGHTS

### Old Town
Today's old town is one of the most beautiful and unusual in all of Turkey. Between 1918-1939, the town was part of the French-administered, mandated territory of Syria, and it retains a mixture of French provincial charm and Arabian romance.

### Cave Church of St Peter
Saints Peter, Paul and Barnabus are said to have preached in this cave to the Christian population of Antioch. It was the first Christian church and was embellished with a Gothic façade by crusaders in the 13th century.

### Turkish money

Without wishing to disparage the Turkish Lira, the fact remains that many traders in the big town bazaars prefer to deal in the main western currencies. You are in a better position to haggle if you are bargaining with foreign currency, and the same can be said of the small hotels. So remember to travel with some pounds or dollars in your pocket. As for local currency, it's always best to acquire your Turkish Lira in Turkey, as you get a better exchange rate here than you do back home.

*Open daily (except Mon) 08.00-12.00 and 13.30-18.00 hrs; Entrance approx. 40p; a little outside the main town, via the Süreya Halefoğlu Cad.*

## MUSEUM

### Arkeoloji Müzesi
### (Archaeological Museum)
★ This museum houses the largest collection of Roman mosaics in the world, dating back to the 2nd and 3rd centuries AD.

*Roman mosaic from the Archaeological Museum at Antakya*

Most of them were discovered on sites or in villas of the surrounding area and depict mythological scenes. Nearly all of them are intact and their colours are just as bright as they ever were. There is also a collection of Roman coins and items of jewellery.
*Daily 09.00-12.00 and 13.00-18.00 hrs; Mon 13.00-18.00 hrs; Entrance approx. £2; Çekmece Cad.*

## RESTAURANTS

This is one of the best places to be if you have a real penchant for kebabs. The *meze* on offer in restaurants are nearly always deli-cious. Try the Arabic version of humus (a creamy dip made from chick-peas) which is spicier than the humus we are familiar with.

### Anadolu Restoran
Large selection of starters, fish and kebabs. Pleasant service.
*Saray Cad. 50; Category 3*

## HOTELS

### Atahan Hotel
Small hotel with Arabic atmosphere.
*28 rooms; Hürriyet Cad. 28; Category 3; Tel: 326/214 21 40*

### Büyük Antakya
The best and most beautiful hotel in the town, with European-style luxury and nightclub.
*72 rooms; Atatürk Cad. 8; Category 1; Tel:326/213 58 60*

## INFORMATION

### Turizm Danişma Bürosu
*Atatürk Cad.; Tel: 326/216 06 10*

## SURROUNDING AREA

### Harbiye (Daphne's Grove)   (F4)
✿ ❀ Celebrations in honour of the dead have been held here since time immemorial. Legend has it that Daphne was pursued here by Apollo and that, in order to escape the god's attentions, she turned herself into a laurel tree. Today's site has lost something of its romanticism. The grove is a popular day-trip destination and has suffered as a consequence. But don't let this put you off. Admire, instead, the many surrounding waterfalls – best seen from the inside of a restaurant!
*9 km south of Antakya*

# Practical information

*Important addresses and other useful information
for your visit to Turkey*

## ACTIVITY HOLIDAYS

There is no shortage of choice for those looking for something sporty or adventurous to do on their holiday: yachting, diving, rafting, windsurfing, fishing, golfing, caving, skiing, mountaineering and trekking. Ask your travel agent or consult the Sunday broadsheets for details about tour operators specializing in activity holidays. Alternatively, contact the tourist information office at home or in Turkey.

## AIR TRAVEL (DOMESTIC FLIGHTS)

Turkish Airlines (*Türk Hava Yolları*, or THY) operates a service between Adana, Ankara, Antalya, Dalaman, Diyarbakır, Elazığ, Erzurum, Kayseri, Istanbul, Izmir, Malatya, Samsun, Sivas, Trabzon and Van. Prices for a single journey range between £25 and £65.

## BANKS

All banks exchange foreign currency and accept both Traveller's Cheques and Eurocheques.
*Opening times Mon-Fri 09.00-12.00* and *13.30-17.00 hrs.* The larger banks and many of the hotels, restaurants and shops in the major resorts also accept credit cards, while automatic cash dispensers can be found in all the main towns. In the smaller towns, however, credit cards are not commonly accepted.

## BUSES

Coaches are the most popular and practical means of transport in Turkey and fares are very cheap. There is a dense network of private bus companies that run regular long-distance services, day and night, between the big towns. They are generally very comfortable but be prepared for the loud music that will accompany you on your journey. Tickets can be booked on the spot from the local bus station (*otogar* or *garajlar*).

## CAMPING

Camping is unrestricted in Turkey, but you are advised by the Ministry of Culture and Tourism to camp on the sites operated by the Mocamp-Karavan chain. For further information contact: *Kervanseray AS, PK 211 şişli/Istanbul.*

There are a number of well-maintained and attractive camp-sites all along the coast. They are open from April/May through until October. Bear in mind, though, that the little pensions are often cheaper to stay in than the campsites.

## CAR HIRE

All the large car-hire firms have offices in Istanbul and Ankara, as well as in the major tourist resorts on the western and southern coasts. If you want to hire a car for an extended period, it's advisable to book one prior to your departure, as you'll find long-term car hire is more expensive once you get to Turkey. However, if you just want to hire a car for a day trip, there are plenty of Turkish firms offering reasonable rates. Just make sure that you check the condition of the car beforehand.

## CUSTOMS

There are no limits imposed on foreign and Turkish currency brought into the country, although you are advised to declare large sums and to keep all your exchange receipts. Duty-free limits are as follows: 200 cigarettes; 50 cigars; 5 litres of alcohol. If you are driving across the border, your car will be given a stamp of approval in your passport. This is to ensure that you leave the country in the same vehicle. The exportation of antiques over 100 years old is strictly forbidden and customs officials are by no means lenient with offenders. If you

have bought a new carpet, make sure you acquire some proof of purchase for it.

## DRIVING

The Turks have a reputation for reckless driving, so be alert and remember to keep to the right-hand side of the road; and always give priority to the right, especially on roundabouts. If you are involved in a road accident, you must get a report from the police before any insurance claim can be dealt with by the loss adjuster. You are strongly recommended to take out personal accident insurance and a collision damage waiver, in addition to third party insurance, which is compulsory. The speed limits are 50 km/h in towns, and 90 km/h in open areas. The Turkish Touring and Automobile Club can assist you in the case of a break down.
*Istanbul Head Office Tel: (212) 282 81 40, Fax: (212) 282 80 42*

## ELECTRICITY

Current is 220 volts.

## EMBASSIES & CONSULATES

### Britain
*Meşrutiyet Cad., 34, Tepebaşi/Beyo-glu, Istanbul; Tel: (212) 293 75 40, Fax: (212) 245 49 89*

### USA
*Meşrutiyet Cad., 104-108, Tepebaşi Istanbul; Tel: (212) 251 36 02, Fax: (212) 251 36 32*

There are also British consulates in Ankara, Antalya, Bodrum, Izmir, Marmaris and Mersin, and American consulates in Adana and Izmir.

## EMERGENCIES

In case of emergency the police can be contacted on 155, the ambulance service on 112 and the fire brigade on 110.

## INFORMATION

**Turkish Information Office in UK:**
*1st Floor, 170-173 Piccadilly, London W1V 9DD; Tel: 0171-629 7771, Fax: 0171-491 07 73, E-Mail: eb 25 @cityscape.co.uk*

**Turkish Information Office in USA:**
*821 United Nations Plaza New York, NY 10017; Tel: (212) 687 2194, Fax: (212) 599 75 68, E-Mail: http : //WWW.turkey.org/turkey*

## MEDICAL CARE

If you need a doctor, ask at your hotel, or at the Tourist Information Office. Pharmacies (*Eczane*) are available everywhere, but you're advised to bring basic emergency medication with you. Make sure that your travel insurance includes medical cover.

## NEWSPAPERS

You can find most of the English national dailies on sale in the big towns and resorts. The 'Turkish Daily News', the local English language newspaper, is also widely distributed.

## PASSPORTS/VISAS

British, Irish and American nationals who enter Turkey require a visa for a stay of up to 3 months. A sticker visa, which costs around £5/$7.50, can be acquired at the border gates.

## PETROL

You'll find there is no shortage of petrol (*benzin*) stations along the main routes and more and more garages in Turkey have lead-free petrol (*kursunsuz benzin*). The Turkish Tourist Office can supply you with a list of such garages.

## PHOTOGRAPHY

Taking photographs in Turkey poses few problems, but exercise discretion in the smaller more remote villages. Taking pictures of military installations is forbidden. Films are expensive here, so you should stock up before leaving.

## POST & TELEPHONE

Post offices, or PTTs, can be found in most places, including the smaller towns and villages. The Turkish postal service is very reliable and the larger post offices now offer a fax service. The cost of postage is more or less in line with EC rates. Stamps can only be bought in post offices and telephone tokens and phone cards are also available from the counter. You can place direct calls abroad from most places – bear in mind that phone-calls from Turkey are not cheap. Phone cards are more convenient for international calls. To telephone abroad, dial 00 first and wait for the dialling tone. Then dial the relevant international code: United Kingdom 44, United States and Canada 1, Ireland 353. If you encounter problems getting a direct line, you can go via the operator in the local post office.
*Opening times: Mon-Fri, 08.30-12.30 and 13.30-17.30 hrs. The main*

*post offices are also open on Sunday from 09.00-19.00 hrs.*

## TIME DIFFERENCE

Turkish time is GMT plus 2 hours. Remember that flight timetables are always based on local time.

## TRAINS

Turkish State Railways (TCDD) has a wide network which connects most major cities. Unfortunately the system does not run that efficiently, having remained largely undeveloped since the 1950s.

## WATER QUALITY

Tests carried out all-year-round indicate that the sea-water off the bathing beaches along the Turkish Riviera has an excellent level of cleanliness. Leading the way in hygiene are Alanya, Antalya and Side.

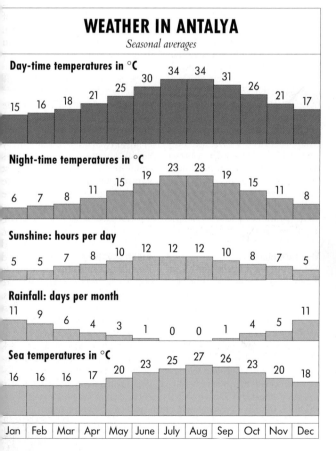

## WEATHER IN ANTALYA
*Seasonal averages*

**Day-time temperatures in °C**

| Jan | Feb | Mar | Apr | May | June | July | Aug | Sep | Oct | Nov | Dec |
|-----|-----|-----|-----|-----|------|------|-----|-----|-----|-----|-----|
| 15 | 16 | 18 | 21 | 25 | 30 | 34 | 34 | 31 | 26 | 21 | 17 |

**Night-time temperatures in °C**

| Jan | Feb | Mar | Apr | May | June | July | Aug | Sep | Oct | Nov | Dec |
|-----|-----|-----|-----|-----|------|------|-----|-----|-----|-----|-----|
| 6 | 7 | 8 | 11 | 15 | 19 | 23 | 23 | 19 | 15 | 11 | 8 |

**Sunshine: hours per day**

| Jan | Feb | Mar | Apr | May | June | July | Aug | Sep | Oct | Nov | Dec |
|-----|-----|-----|-----|-----|------|------|-----|-----|-----|-----|-----|
| 5 | 5 | 7 | 8 | 10 | 12 | 12 | 12 | 10 | 8 | 7 | 5 |

**Rainfall: days per month**

| Jan | Feb | Mar | Apr | May | June | July | Aug | Sep | Oct | Nov | Dec |
|-----|-----|-----|-----|-----|------|------|-----|-----|-----|-----|-----|
| 11 | 9 | 6 | 4 | 3 | 1 | 0 | 0 | 1 | 4 | 5 | 11 |

**Sea temperatures in °C**

| Jan | Feb | Mar | Apr | May | June | July | Aug | Sep | Oct | Nov | Dec |
|-----|-----|-----|-----|-----|------|------|-----|-----|-----|-----|-----|
| 16 | 16 | 16 | 17 | 20 | 23 | 25 | 27 | 26 | 23 | 20 | 18 |

# Do's and Don'ts

*How to avoid some of the traps and pitfalls
the unwary traveller may face*

### Cheap car hire

As a general rule, you should hire cars from reputable international firms. Although they are much more costly than their Turkish counterparts, they do offer a safer package, particularly with regard to insurance. If you have an accident when driving a car hired from a Turkish firm, you may find that the insurance contract included in the hire charge does not provide sufficient cover. Many travel agents offer fly/drive package deals which are good value for money and save you the worry of finding a car on arrival.

### Cut-price coaches

When buying a bus ticket for an extended journey, you'll find that prices vary a great deal between the different private bus companies. Check which company appears to run the most buses in the area you are in. The Pamukkale company, for example, has a good reputation. As a rule, the more expensive, the better. A higher priced ticket will ensure a seat on a comfortable coach, good service and, above all, better working conditions for the driver. This is very important, as you can be confident of a greater degree of safety. Most of the coach accidents in Turkey happen because the driver is over-tired.

### Group shopping

Regular complaints are made about tour guides who take the

---

### The Fainting Imam

This expression has a lot less to do with religion than one might assume – 'The imam has fainted' (Turkish: *Imam bayildi*) is the wonderful name of a typical vegetable dish made of aubergines stuffed with onions and tomatoes. The story goes that the expression was coined after a miserly Muslim priest fainted upon seeing his wife use a whole litre of olive oil in the preparation of the poor man's meal. Despite commonly-held preconceptions, however, good Turkish food does not swim in oil.

*Browsing in the souvenir markets is a great way to spend the morning*

groups in their charge to particular places to shop. This isn't necessarily a bad thing, as the shop which the guide chooses will have been carefully selected. It would not be in their interest to take clients to any retail outlet that deals in poor quality goods. Of course the guides, or coach drivers, get certain perks for this 'service'. The shops pay them a commission which can sometimes be as high as 30% of the price of the goods sold. This inevitably raises the prices, so you should either be prepared to pay a little extra for the convenience of buying something on the spot without any fuss, or else you can visit other shops of your own choosing, but be prepared to spend more time checking quality and comparing prices.

## Lengthy train journeys

The Turkish rail network has been notoriously neglected since the 1950s and if you're going on a long journey, you should travel by bus or plane wherever possble. Not only are these more comfortable and reliable forms of transport, they are also exceptionally cheap.

## Steep bills

Few things are more unpleasant at the end of a meal than receiving an expensive bill which in no way reflects the quality of the food you have eaten. Bear in mind that, especially in seaside fish restaurants, you may well be paying extra for the view. To avoid any misunderstanding, confirm prices before ordering.

## Street noise

Unwelcome noise levels can be a problem even in expensive hotels. Ask to see the room before booking so that you can check whether it overlooks a main street, and find out if there's a nightclub or any other potential source of noise in the area.

## The Turkish pest

The *korsan*, or 'Turkish pest', is a regular feature of the retail trade. Whether inviting you for a cup of tea or loitering at the entrance of an ancient site, informing you that the place has unfortunately just closed for the day, the chances are that you will end up being lured into his brother's carpet shop! If you are not interested, the best policy is to ignore them.

93

# What do you get for your money?

 The currency of Turkey is the Turkish Lira (TL). Bank notes come in denominations of 10 000; 20 000; 50 000; 100 000; 200 000; 250 000; 500 000; and 1 000 000 TL, and there are coins of 500, 2500 and 5000 TL. Turkey's galloping inflation makes it impossible to quote a reliable exchange rate – you can find out the actual rate from banks or by checking the newspapers prior to departure. It's always cheaper to exchange money once you get to Turkey and there's no limit imposed on the amount of foreign and Turkish currency you may bring in. You can exchange up to $5000 (around £3400) in banks and through other exchange facilities. Eurocheques can be cashed on the spot, as can Traveller's cheques. Remember to retain the exchange receipt, as you have to present this when you need to change any Turkish currency you have left before going home. The limit imposed on Turkish currency which can be taken out of the country is $5000.

Because Turkey has a floating exchange rate policy, tourists are not affected by inflation.

On the whole, the cost of living in Turkey is much cheaper than it is in Western Europe. To give you an idea of how things compare, here are a few rough price indications: a domestic flight from Istanbul to Antalya, costs around £52/$78 and a single journey by coach between these towns would cost in the region of £6.50/$9.75. Public transport, petrol and entrance into the sites are all cheap. Entry into museums is generally about £1.50/$2.25 per person and in very few cases does it greatly exceed this amount. A glass of tea costs around 13p/20c, and lunch in a good restaurant including *mezeler*, salad, a glass of wine, mineral water and bread will set you back between £4.30/$6.50 and £6.50/$9.75 per person. Dinner, even in an expensive fish restaurant, will always be cheaper than in an equivalent restaurant in Western Europe. Hotels are, as a rule, very good value